The Intertidal Wilderness

ANNE WERTHEIM

SIERRA CLUB BOOKS · SAN FRANCISCO

The Sierra Club, founded in 1892 by John Muir, has devoted itself to the study and protection of the earth's scenic and ecological resources—mountains, wetlands, woodlands, wild shores and rivers, deserts and plains. The publishing program of the Sierra Club offers books to the public as a nonprofit educational service in the hope that they may enlarge the public's understanding of the Club's basic concerns. The point of view expressed in each book, however, does not necessarily represent that of the Club. The Sierra Club has some fifty chapters coast to coast, in Canada, Hawaii, and Alaska. For information about how you may participate in its programs to preserve wilderness and the quality of life, please address inquiries to Sierra Club, 730 Polk Street, San Francisco, CA 94109.

LIBRARY OF CONGRESS CATALOGING IN PUBLICATION DATA

Wertheim, Anne.
The intertidal wilderness.

Bibliography: p.
Includes index.
1. Intertidal ecology—Pacific Coast (North America)
2. Intertidal ecology.   I. Title.
QH95.3.W47 1985   574.5'2638   84-22220
ISBN 0-87156-839-X
ISBN 0-87156-831-4 (pbk.)

Book and jacket design by Wilsted & Taylor
Composition by Wilsted & Taylor

Printed by Dai Nippon Printing Company, Ltd., Tokyo, Japan

10 9 8 7 6 5 4 3 2

Contents

ACKNOWLEDGMENTS

I would like to express a special thanks to the following people who were involved in the genesis or preparation of this
book.

To Ann O'Hanlon, who nurtured and encouraged my visual interests, goes a continuing and deep affection.

Special acknowledgments go to Mr. Nixon Griffis for his
unhesitating interest in this book project and the generous
support that he and the American Littoral Society provided.

The new Nikon camera systems were wonderfully accu-
rate for photographing tidepools. Thanks go to Cathy Gouch
and Mike Phillips at Nikon, Inc., for the generous loan of
equipment.

Warm thanks to Laura Shapiro, Egbert G. Leigh, and Alan
J. Kohn for their time in reading the manuscript; their view-
points and interpretations, which enhanced it; and their ad-
vice, which improved both the accuracy and the writing. I
would also like to thank Megan N. Dethier, Judy Diamond,
Allison R. Palmer, Robert S. Steneck, and Kenneth P. Sebens
for their contributions.

It is with deep appreciation that I recognize Ann Diamond,
Mary Alanson Powell, Lila and Neville Rich, William M.
Roth, Alice Rusell-Shapiro, Cornelia Wattley, Evelyn and
Fred Wertheim, and the Richard and Rhoda Goldman Fund,
whose generous gifts made this book possible.

Finally, my thanks go to Robert T. Paine, without whose
expertise, enthusiasm, and unflagging help this book would
never have been written.

CHAPTER ONE

Introduction

As long as there has been ocean there has been an intertidal zone. An intertidal zone, by definition the narrow belt lying between the highest and lowest tidemarks, is an "edge" that marks the interface between two very different realms: land and sea. Like many other biological edges it can be extremely rich. One finds there not only an astounding variety of plants and animals, but also images in color, form, and texture woven layer upon layer. At the more exposed, wave-swept rocky shores along the outer coast, such as those that are the subject of this book, the landscape is hazardous but also more vivid and more varied than those shores in protected areas.

Tidal waters alternately submerge and reveal this landscape, at low tide allowing an expanded view of the shore and the myriad of organisms living there. During low tide one can venture out onto this terrain and wander within the seemingly providential pause in the ocean's surge. Soon the tidal waters return, modifying or rearranging the exquisite detail of this drama, and refreshing the participants. Each new tide reasserts the contrast between the cosmic proportions of tidal events and the finer organic details.

The Pacific coast of North America offers the richest intertidal habitat in the temperate zone, north or south. Several factors contribute to this cornucopia: the upwelling of the nutrient-rich bottom waters just offshore, which fertilizes both the plankton and bottom-dwelling plants; a freedom from ice that elsewhere abrades the shore, and from freezes, which can wipe out resident plants and animals; the frequent coastal fogs in the summertime, which protect the shore from the sun's heat; and the near absence, for reasons that continue to mystify ecologists, of herbivorous fishes.

I have focused this essay on the west coast of North America, where many of the common species are ubiquitous and extend from northern Baja California to the limits of the Gulf of Alaska. Even minimum familiarity with the intertidal plants and especially the animals allows one to feel at home throughout this great latitudinal range. The intertidal is replete with striking patterns and subtle, seemingly endless variations on some common themes. An understanding of the underlying causal processes allows one to interpret many of these patterns. This book presents some of these patterns and, where possible, illustrates the dynamic processes that generate them. What first draws one to the shore is its beauty, yet a little knowledge serves to highlight the visual splendor and to emphasize the awesome, harmonious forces at play in the design of nature.

Organisms are not haphazardly distributed along the shore, but rather are arranged in distinct bands, or zones, parallel to it. The rhythm of the tides leads one to think that the higher zones must be occupied by organisms more resistant to the prolonged absence of water, and that three primary factors might govern the distribution and zonation of intertidal organisms: the strength of waves (or, conversely, the degree of shelter from the surf), the nature of the surface on which the organisms can grow (rock, cobble, or sand, and if rock, its textural qualities and degree of hardness), and the relative proportion of time spent exposed to water or air. As marine biology has evolved as a science, biologists have learned to check their ideas on distribution through experiments, and they have turned their attention to how the different animals and plants on the seashore affect each other and restrict each other's distributions. It is now commonly believed that the lower distributional limits of many intertidal organisms are set by biological factors—other animals or plants, which either displace or eat them—while physical factors—the prolonged absence from water, and risk of overheating or desiccation—set the upper limits. The time may come when we discover that biological factors are of major significance to both distributional extremes for all but the highest species.

PLATE 1. *Wave-Swept Rocky Shore*

Plate 1 shows the rocky outer coast at the northwest tip of Washington State. One of the unusual features of the west coast of North America is that for enormous geographic stretches the outer coast is primarily composed of solid rock. Thus, the larvae of rocky shore organisms find a large target on which to settle. In contrast, the east coast of North America, especially south of Cape Cod, is predominantly sandy, and the spatially limited rocky habitat is relatively poor in species. Although most of my photographs were taken in Washington State, some are from California and Alaska, and they represent the suite of conspicuous plants and animals whose geographic range is two to three thousand miles of Pacific coast.

PLATE 2A. *High Tide*
PLATE 2B. *Low Tide*

Plates 2a and 2b are of an intertidal zone at both high and low tide. Along the Pacific coast of North America, four tides occur per day— two highs and two lows, each usually of different amplitude. Simply speaking, tides are a result of gravitational pulls of the sun and the moon on the earth's oceans (see the Appendix, page 134 for information on tide tables). *Intertidal zone* is a general address, and all the organisms that live there share certain processes and problems attendant to staying alive. One could write a more precise address, and indeed the intertidal is a conglomeration of innumerable habitats, including nooks, crannies, crevices, rock walls, surge channels, and tidepools, each with subtly different features and therefore different as a place to live.

4

PLATE 1

PLATE 3. *Kelp and Sea Grass*

The intertidal brown alga *Laminaria setchellii* (plate 3) belongs to a productive plant group commonly referred to as kelps. Also in the plate is the green sea grass *Phyllospadix scouleri*, which often forms intertidal meadows.

One measure of the extreme significance of nearshore habitats is their contribution to the production of plant matter. Although algal beds, reefs, and estuaries occupy only half of 1 percent of the total world ocean area, they contribute a disproportionately high 7 percent of the net primary production (new organic matter produced by photosynthesis), thus serving as the truck farms of the sea.

Laminaria setchellii produces annual growth rings, which are easily counted when the alga is cross-sectioned: the plants may be four to twenty years old. Other intertidal organisms that have been marked and followed through time also attain considerable age: barnacles 1 centimeter across may be twelve to thirteen years old; and one giant green sea anemone was kept in captivity for seventy years. Calculations suggest that in their natural habitat many sea anemones are at least five hundred years old. Most people do not appreciate the longevity of many of the organisms, nor the importance this bears for the community as a whole. Species that attain great ages and that may take more than a year to mature sexually have lost the ecological capacity to respond rapidly to changes in their environment, and special care must be taken for their preservation.

PLATE 4. *The Kelp* Laminaria setchellii

PLATE 3

PLATE 4

PLATE 5 . *Wave Action*

The ocean's surge is an integral part of the daily lives of intertidal organisms. All these organisms require water and waves to keep them moist, supply oxygen, bring food, and remove wastes. But while they are dependent upon the ocean, many eventually succumb to it: mussels may die from being swept away, and other organisms may be buried in water-borne sediment.

The formidable forces of moving and breaking water (plate 5) can pose substantial challenges and hazards to intertidal organisms. Biological adaptations to minimize the risks to life in wave-swept conditions pervade the design features of many species. Shell shape, body size, and the relative flexibility of the stalks and stems of attached plants and animals, for instance, are all related to contending with the stresses imposed by waves.

Where strong wave action occurs on exposed shores, one generally finds a much broader, lusher intertidal area than in a calm, protected area with an equivalent tidal displacement. By throwing and splashing water higher than it would go as a result of tidal movement alone, wave action increases the amount of rock surface that is habitable for intertidal life. Thus, on very exposed shores, the upper limit to marine life can be 10 to 30 feet above the predicted tidal limits. In contrast, in those rare protected habitats where the water creeps in and out with barely a ripple, one rarely finds marine life extending even to the tidal limit.

PLATE 5

9

PLATE 6. *Seascape*

PLATE 7. *Intertidal Diversity*

Part of both the esthetic and biological attraction of the intertidal is the enormous diversity of species living on the shore. As one moves from high to low levels in the intertidal zone, the assemblage becomes even richer and more varied, and the lowest levels might be called a phylogenetic sampler. Often as many animal phyla are represented in 1 square meter of intertidal as exist in the entire terrestrial realm. At least seven phyla help compose plate 7: starfish (Echinodermata), anemones and hydroids (Cnidaria), and tunicates (Chordata) are especially conspicuous.

These organisms have evolved from the ancestral multicellular animals that in ancient times and seas evolved from primordial cells. The animals are classified into main groups, called phyla, and the plants into divisions, according to similarities and differences that reflect evolutionary and structural relationships, not superficial appearances. Basic elements of body design, such as type of symmetry, organization of cells and tissue layers from which the body is formed, organ system development, and similarities in embryo structure, can all be important in classifying animals. Plant taxonomy is partly based on the knowledge of pigments, some of which mask the presence of others. For a

PLATE 6

PLATE 7

11

more detailed description of phylogenetic relationships, see Appendix. This table gives the classification for two common seashore animals.

Classification	Mussel	Green sea anemone
Kingdom	Animalia	Animalia
Phylum	Mollusca	Cnidaria
Class	Bivalvia	Anthozoa
Order	Mytiloidea	Actinaria
Family	Mytilidae	Actiniidae
Genus	Mytilus	Anthopleura
Species	Mytilus californianus	Anthopleura xanthogrammica

In the Latin binomial names used in this book—for example *Mytilus californianus*—the second element, or species name, is the most exact identification that can be given. Species are groups of actually or potentially interbreeding natural populations, but as with individuals in the genus and species to which humanity belongs, *Homo sapiens*, members can vary considerably in behavior, appearance, or ecology. Sometimes which species an organism belongs to is unclear. Where this is the case, the organism will be identified in this book by its generic name only, followed by the abbreviation for species, *sp.*

PLATE 8. *Middle to high intertidal algae, including* Analipus japonicus *and* Iridaea cornucopiae, *some of which are parched due to long periods of exposure to sun and lack of immersion by waves.*

PLATE 9. *Middle intertidal algae, including* Leathesia difformis, Ulva *sp.,* Halosaccion glandiforme, Porphyra *sp.,* Microcladia *sp., barnacles, and sea anemones.*

PLATE 8

PLATE 9

PLATE 10. *Rock Wall at an Exposed Site*

Especially conspicuous in plate 10, of an exposed shore at Tatoosh Is., Washington, are a ubiquitous starfish, *Pisaster ochraceus*, mussels, *Mytilus californianus*, barnacles, *Balanus glandula*, and brown alga, *Laminaria setchellii*. These, and some of the associated species, are also characteristic of Southeast Alaska and northern Baja California, which suggests their enormous geographic range.

In this photograph it is clear that the mobile organisms are not equally common and the sessile residents occupy dissimilar amounts of space. Throughout this book I refer to the ecological properties of populations or ensembles of populations in terms of distribution, abundance, or diversity. For marine intertidal organisms the term *distribution* contains three primary dimensions: the range of a species at geographic scales, especially where physical harshness or barriers determine latitudinal or longitudinal limits; the bathymetric distribution—that is, how far above and below the zero tide datum a particular species may be found; and the fine details of an individual's spatial position, such as microenvironments in which only certain species are found.

Abundance is simply an expression of whether a species is common or rare. When quantified, abundance is expressed as number of individuals per square meter, the percentage of an area occupied by some particular population, or the living weight of some species per unit area.

Diversity is an ecological measure that can be either qualitative or quantitative and that reflects the numbers of species inhabiting the same environment and therefore potentially interacting. It can also refer to the abundances of the different species present.

PLATE 10

15

PLATE II. *Starfish and Goose Barnacles*

Plate II depicts an interaction between two species: the starfish *Pisaster ochraceus* attacking a gooseneck barnacle, *Pollicipes polymerus*. By eating goose barnacles, starfish can keep the lower intertidal free of them, thus helping to maintain zonation patterns (see plate 32a and plate 32b).

An *interaction* occurs when two organisms of the same or different species act on each other in some way. In order to interpret such interactions I have relied on a growing scientific literature in ecology. The evidence gathered by three different methods is important in the science of ecology: sampling, observing, and experimenting. To understand intertidal zonation, one must find out how many of each different kind of organism live in what kinds of places; this can be accomplished by sampling. Then one must look at the animals and plants more closely, to see what the animals eat, how their prey respond, when the organisms reproduce, and when the young appear. But, observation alone has proven inadequate to detect the causes of intertidal zonation or to evaluate the ecological roles of individual species in natural assemblages.

Ecologists have begun to understand these natural processes by tampering on a very small scale with the order of nature through experimentation. When such manipulations are scientifically planned, they are based on a comparison between an unaltered site left in its natural state (this is called a control) and another site, manipulated in some specific fashion. For instance, such experiments may involve the exclusion or addition of some specific predator or competitor, the addition or deletion of refuges, minor modifications of anatomical structures, and even changes in the substratum's color. When properly executed and repeated, such experiments generate precise knowledge of the interactive nature of communities or of how the population of one kind of species is affected by the presence or absence of another. This information is also critically important in managing seashore communities, in predicting the possible effects of human intervention, and in

PLATE I I

17

accelerating a community's recovery. Many of the references in the section headed "Further Reading" refer to such experiments and show how ecologists have reached some of their conclusions about natural patterns and processes.

PLATE 12A. *Oiled Murre* Uria aalge
PLATE 12B. *Dumping in the Intertidal Zone*
PLATE 12C. *Destruction of Mussel Bed*

Threats to the health and future of the shore are increasing at an alarming rate. The disfigurements in plates 12a, 12b, and 12c are tantamount to vandalism in the largest sense, and should alert us to the dangers of dumping toxic chemicals and wastes, oil spills and harmful detergents used to clean them up, myriad other effects of industrialization, and the overexploitation of some species plus the introduction of others that might be difficult to keep in check.

The rocky intertidal is only one of many habitats in danger on the coast's margins. Others under comparable pressures are estuaries, marshes, lagoons, bays, beaches, and even cliffs. These environments are open in the sense that they have no clear-cut physical boundaries. Thus they can share a pool of widely dispersing propagules (spores, seeds, or planktonic larvae) and pollutants, and are subject to influences from both land and sea. Some of these anthropogenic effects are obvious, but others are much more subtle and therefore easy to misinterpret. From the standpoint of regulation or preservation the problem is enormous, for individual species often reside in different habitats according to their life-history phase, or depend on nutrients generated many leagues away. Moreover, most species are vulnerable to inimical influences produced beyond national boundaries and transported shoreward by the vagaries of currents. To date, no solution to such broad environmental problems has been found and the challenge of stewardship has not been met. Appendix C offers a brief intertidal "etiquette," or ethic; anything one does to minimize the inadvertent effects of a journey into the intertidal will help preserve the seashore in its natural state.

The importance of maintaining the integrity and grandeur of the shore cannot be overemphasized, for its intrinsic qualities continue to nurture and sustain our lives. Besides conveying some of the fragility, complexity, and interdependence of the plants and animals that live between the tides along one of the world's most spectacular coastlines, I hope I have portrayed a place with its own special beauty, where gazing into a tidepool brings magic, and where the subtleties are infinite and kaleidoscopic. This planet we inhabit is a watery one; only in the intertidal can we be in the worlds of both land and sea at once. An ethereal and powerful meld of primal elements—solid rock, moving water, and life itself—sometimes enveloped in fog and other times brilliantly alight, the intertidal wilderness will always find a way to stir our senses. Whether or not you have direct access to the shore and its unique beauty, I hope you will see it through this book as a place to find new meaning.

The following chapters illustrate some of the myriad patterns characteristic of exposed shorelines and provide some clues to interpreting the underlying causal processes. When you visit the shore, keep in mind that no two areas are identical in topography or inhabitants. Each intertidal site has a flavor and texture of its own. And just as the composition of species varies from place to place and time to time, so does the relative intensity of and balance between the many interactions that affect adjacent and associated organisms. Remember, too, that you will not see all the intertidal treasures in any one excursion. Some of these things are elusive, others subtle, and an important part of the allure in any wilderness is the prospect of exploration. Most importantly, don't let patterns and scenarios described in these pages stop you from making your own observations on the shore and your own discoveries of its powerful abstract beauty.

PLATE 12C

PLATE 12B

CHAPTER TWO

〜〜〜〜〜〜〜〜〜〜〜〜

Competition: *The Struggle for Limited Resources*

ORGANISMS have similar and overlapping needs for the basic requisites of life: a place to live, secure refuges, adequate food, and in the case of plants, light. If demand for a particular resource exceeds supply, the resource becomes a limiting factor that induces competition. Since this interaction is of basic importance to understanding the subtle dynamics of any rocky shore, it is necessary to make some fundamental distinctions. When members of a single species are vying—for instance, when hermit crabs of the same species compete for shells in which to live—the quarrel is called *intraspecific*. If two or more different species are involved, the competition is *interspecific*.

The competition process itself falls into two major categories, though the distinctions between them are sometimes blurred. When the limiting resource is defended by one of the participants or when any direct contact is made, we are witnessing *interference competition*, the most common mode of intertidal competition. Living space is a resource that can be defended, particularly by sessile, permanently attached, organisms, and most of the competitive interactions described below fall into this category. Moreover, because the limiting resource (space) is easily identified and the organisms are often large and observable, many classic ecological studies on competition have been performed on rocky shores.

The other kind of competitive interaction is called *exploitation competition*, and it involves a mutual striving for a resource that is not defensible. This type occurs, for instance, when one species in the course of depleting its food supply reduces the probability of the other species obtaining it. No direct contact between the participants is necessary, and the more efficient species usually wins eventually. Competition for food by mobile species provides examples of this interaction, the clearest of which involve small organisms inhabiting water columns in the open sea where it is difficult if not impossible to defend the resource.

These definitions refer to ideal conditions and are often applied only with real difficulty to the natural world. For example, on rocky shores, mussels and barnacles live attached to the rock surface and feed on suspended particles brought to them by the water. In this example both food and space are potentially limiting, although marine ecologists generally judge space to be of greater immediate importance, because the organisms can influence its overall availability. In these open communities where large volumes of flowing water continually bring food items to sessile, filter-feeding animals, probably enough for all of them to meet their needs, it is unlikely that competition for food among them is either commonplace or generally important.

Competition has had a potent effect on evolution, influencing organisms' distribution, behavior, morphologies, and reproductive strategies. One way for an animal to avoid competitive destruction is to live somewhere in the intertidal where its competitors cannot survive. This explanation is often invoked where similar species using resources in a comparable fashion do not overlap spatially. Thus, some barnacles live high in the intertidal and others low down. Two or more similar, mobile species that overlap in distribution often eat different prey; this can be observed in nudibranchs. Does this explain their coexistence? Some species are "weedy": they are adept at invading space but once there do not persist. Many examples can be found in seasonally abundant algae. Are they too avoiding competition by being biologically active when a dominant species is inactive?

The evidence of competition for space is easily identified on rocky shores. You might find sharp intraspecific or interspecific boundaries; injured tissue along contact lines between species; interspecific crushing, crowding, undercutting, or overgrowth, as in barnacles. You might also see regular spacing, as though some constant interaction determined the distance between individuals—as with limpets or some large algal species. One has only to examine the underside of an algal holdfast to find a miniature graveyard of other species that have been overgrown. The ability to acquire, usurp, or guard the spatial resource is often easy to recognize in sessile species, since brute force seems to be their primary tactic. It is possible to see clashes between motile species, such as fish or limpets, as well; however, these are difficult to interpret and can express other types of interaction, such as predation.

Ecological wisdom suggests that space is the principal limited resource for many intertidal species. The availability of refuges from predation can also be important, and the influences of varying amounts and kinds of food have barely been examined. Hence there is still room for alternative explanations of the ways numerous species coexist or why some shores are richer in species than others. The following pages show that mutual striving for common resources is observable in rocky intertidal habitats where interference competition tends to be quite graphic.

PLATE 13. *Competition for space between sea anemones* Anthopleura xanthogrammica *and sponge* Haliclona permollis.

PLATE 13

PLATE 1 4 . *Competition for Space*

One striking feature of the rocky intertidal zones of temperate North America's Pacific shores is that most space is occupied. When many different species are using a limited spatial resource, as in plate 14, and the organisms must continue to grow and invade new territory, there is potential for competition. Bare rock and cobbles exist only where powerful scouring and tumbling by waves make them an impossible home or, in still water, where predators and herbivores can work undisturbed by wave action.

PLATE 1 5 . *Typical midshore assemblage in coastal Alaska, showing the chiton* Katharina tunicata, *barnacles* Semibalanus cariosus, *and sponge* Halichondria panicea.

PLATE 14

PLATE 15

PLATE 16A. *Green Algae Atop a Limpet*
PLATE 16B. *Epiphytic Coralline Algae*
PLATE 16C. *Acorn Barnacles on Mussels*

Not only is primary space, the rock substrate, thick with life, but often the organisms themselves are festooned with other plants and animals. Many organisms are secondary-space occupiers either by close association or lack of other or better choices. Plants and animals growing attached to other plants are called *epiphytic*; on animals they are *epizoic*, and a more general term including both is *epibiont*. The well-being of their hosts directly influences their own. Thus, environmental stresses on the host inevitably affect the guest. In plate 16a, the shell of *Notoacmaea scutum* bears tufts of a green filamentous algae, *Cladophora* sp., which can also be found growing on the rock substratum. It is not known whether the alga occupies this mobile habitat as a refuge, as a preferred habitat, or, by necessity, as a suboptimal site. Plate 16b illustrates discs of an epiphytic coralline alga, *Mesophyllum conchatum*, growing on articulated corallines. In this case the relationship appears to be more specific, with the epiphyte restricted to a very limited range of substrata. Plate 16c shows acorn barnacles, small *Balanus* sp., encrusting valves of the mussel *Mytilus californianus*. Although such secondary surfaces are commonplace along our shores, the barnacle's fate is inexorably tied to that of the mussels. Such added risk might suggest why barnacle larvae often choose to settle elsewhere if given a chance.

PLATE 17. *Hermit Crabs*

As part of their life style, hermit crabs require shells. Aggression and ritualized signaling often occur when hermit crabs of the same or different species compete for this limiting resource. The shells they carry serve several essential functions, including protection, for unlike other crabs they have soft abdomens. Their need for bigger homes as they grow continually promotes competitive interactions. In shell contests the smaller of two hermit crabs is made to abandon its shell, allowing the bigger crab to examine its adequacy. Often this is achieved by behavioral signaling, which attains the same end result but minimizes the danger of physical damage to the participants. If the bigger crab wants a new home, a shell exchange will take place. If not, the owners each reclaim their original shells. In plate 17, a *Pagurus* sp., occupying a *Tegula* shell, is initiating an examination of a *Calliostoma* shell inhabited by a smaller member of the same species.

PLATE 18. *Conspicuous in plate 18 are a chiton, sea anemone, barnacles, tunicates, and algae. The photograph shows near total utilization of space in the lower intertidal zone of coastal Alaska, conditions under which competition among species is bound to occur.*

PLATE 17

PLATE 18

PLATE 19A. *Anemone's Aggressive Response*
PLATE 19B. *Clonal Boundary*

Sea anemones have attracted a great deal of attention, for not only do they tend to be large and colorful, but in comparison with other sessile organisms they exhibit a wide range of behaviors. *Anthopleura elegantissima* usually exists as contiguous aggregations of genetically identical individuals, or clones. When alarmed, they will either contract totally or, to defend themselves against intruders, inflate their acrorhagi, special knoblike protuberances equipped with stinging cells. Clone mates aren't aggressive to each other but will use their acrorhagi to injure genetically different individuals. One can often see this aggressive response exhibited in aggregations, as in plate 19a. A subtle feature of intertidal zones where this species abounds is well-demarked borders between adjacent clones. These anemone-free strips, as in plate 19b, once thought to be limpet highways, are now known to be the product of intraspecific competition for space.

33

PLATE 20. *Hydrocoral Territorial Stalemate*

When two sessile organisms come into contact with each other, at least three outcomes are possible. If the individuals are members of the same species they may fuse, as do some sponges; in other circumstances the boundary may remain stable, in a sort of stalemate; or the boundary between two organisms may shift in favor of one or the other, depending on which is the superior competitor. In still another instance, something may come along—a predator perhaps—that changes the entire competitive outcome of the encounter. Plate 20 shows a discrete boundary between two colonies of the hydrocoral *Allopora californica*, each a clone of genetically identical individuals. Such boundaries are commonplace in this species and are thought to be maintained by interclonal aggression. They usually appear to represent a stalemate, with continuity between the clones maintained but neither one successfully overgrowing the other. In general, such boundaries indicate that the resource is being divided, but unless one follows them through time, one can't know what the future holds for either participant.

PLATE 21. *Barnacles*

Barnacles in general show a well-defined hierarchy of competitive abilities, with the larger species in a confrontation crushing, overgrowing, or undercutting the smaller. Don't be surprised, however, if you find reversals. Smaller species will occasionally outcompete a larger one, although these incidents are rare. Plate 21 illustrates some *Balanus glandula* overgrowing individuals of the smaller, browner barnacle *Chthamalus dalli*. In other encounters *B. glandula* appears to have modified its usually circular outline and grown around the *Chthamalus*. Perhaps the differences result from variations in individual size at the time of initial contact.

At other places along the shore, one can find hummocks of *Balanus* sp. When these animals are numerous and space is at a premium, the crowding individuals inadvertently squeeze one another, becoming more columnar in shape as they grow. Individual barnacles characterized by this unstable growth form are more susceptible to being swept off the rocks.

PLATE 20

PLATE 21

PLATES 22A AND 22B. *Mussel Bed, Mytilus californianus, and detail with limpet, hermit crab, and brittle stars.*

On the exposed shores of the Pacific Northwest, the dominant midintertidal competitor is the mussel *Mytilus californianus*. Left to their own devices, without interruption or interference from physical disturbance or predation, mussels are capable of monopolizing the primary substratum by smothering other primary-space occupiers, rendering the space uninhabitable to more mobile species, or presenting a phalanx of sharp edges against which waves shred competing kelps.

Mussels have a means of attachment called a *byssus*, fibers secreted by a gland at the base of the foot. These slender, flexible threads can be voluntarily dissolved by the mussel and new fiber produced, giving mussels the mobility necessary both to move onto new space and to reclaim terrain lost to the ravages of physical disturbance. This ability might explain the competitive dominance of mussels in many rocky intertidal communities worldwide.

Mussel beds can grow up to 40 centimeters thick, are composed of many strata, and make of the habitat an enormously variegated and reticulated world of sheltered openings. This specialized habitat is sufficient to supply space to a seemingly endless number of hangers-on, many of which are too small to be easily seen. Organic debris and fecal matter accumulate here as well, providing a rich soup for deposit and suspension feeders.

As the mussels defeat other organisms by their large size, they become more vulnerable to the shearing forces of wave action. No organism in any natural community can survive as a jack of all trades, master of none; therefore if a species excels in one vital ecological function, a vulnerability elsewhere can be assumed.

A mussel monoculture sharply illustrates the importance of semantics to ecology. With bare space as the reference point, one would call an unbroken stand of relatively large animals, such as mussels, a monoculture, since this life form would appear to be excluding others. On the other hand, if one's frame of reference were the mussel bed, it and its associated community would be described biologically as an extremely rich assemblage.

PLATE 23A. *Sponge, Barnacles, and Coralline Algae*
PLATE 23B. *Sponge and Bryozoa*

Plate 23a illustrates a hierarchical arrangement of species, with the sponge *Halichondria* sp. overgrowing the barnacle *Semibalanus cariosus*, and both of these overgrowing two kinds of crustose coralline algae. Within the latter the darker purple crust, *Pseudolithophyllum muricatum*, is overgrowing the very thin species *Pseudolithophyllum whidbeyense*. Such hierarchical competitive arrangements would soon lead to spatial monopolies were it not for a multiplicity of factors mitigating against the dominant species.

However, straightforward interpretation is often clouded by competitive reversals, as shown in plate 23b. In this situation most of the space is occupied by the bryozoan *Cryptosula* sp. and the sponge *Haliclona permollis*, each of which can be seen overgrowing the other.

One of the issues of interest to marine biologists today is whether competitive interactions are linear and their outcomes predictable, as in the hierarchy in plate 23a, or whether they are arranged in complex networks or loops, with no single species being the winner for more than a relatively brief instant because the relationships are constantly in flux. In networks of competition, all species persist because no one species is capable of dominating all the others.

PLATE 24. *Hydrocoral and Coralline Algae*

The intertidal habitat is unique in many ways. As noted in the introduction, the organisms living there are alternately submerged and emersed by the tide. Another feature that gives the intertidal a flavor of its own is that one finds animals in vigorous competition for space with plants, an interaction not commonly found in the terrestrial world. Plate 60 (page 99) shows the holdfast of the sea palm, *Postelsia palmaeformis*, successfully overgrowing barnacles, mussels, and smaller algae. Plate 24 shows *Pseudolithophyllum muricatum*, the most vigorous competitor amongst the coralline algae, overgrowing the bright pink, pitted skeletons of the colonial animal *Allopora californica*. However, the relationships between the hydrocoral *Allopora* and other species of coralline algae are less clear.

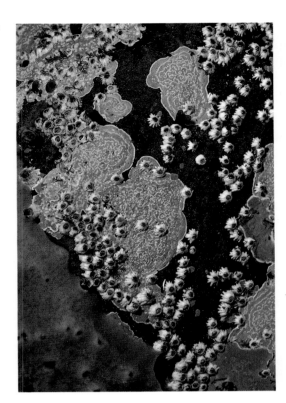

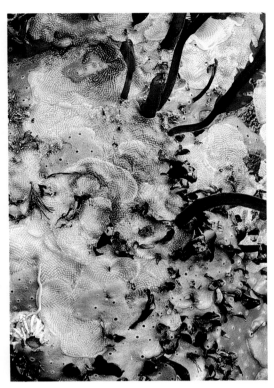

PLATE 24

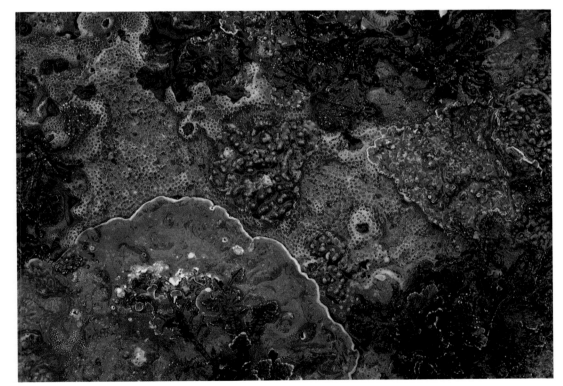

PLATE 25. *Sponge and Barnacles*

Overgrowth relationships are not always antagonistic. Some interactions between two or more species living together in close physical proximity benefit all parties. Or, if only one gains, it will be at no cost to the others. Such relationships have traditionally been termed *mutualisms* or *symbioses*. They have always caught the eye of both naturalists and ecologists, whom they continue to vex.

A fine example is provided by the barnacle *Balanus nubilus* and the sponge *Halichondria panicea*, often associated, as in plate 25. *B. nubilus* is one of the largest acorn barnacles on the west coast of North America and normally is subtidal, but it may grow intertidally on wave-exposed points. *H. panicea*, distinguished by both its odor and texture, has a cosmopolitan distribution and varies in both shape and color. Each can apparently exist without the other.

Substantial experimental evidence indicates that sponges benefit their hosts. We know that sponge cover markedly reduces the ability of tube feet to adhere and thus can reduce predation by starfish, but does the barnacle do anything to attract the sponge? For the sponge, what advantages are conferred other than a suitable settlement site? Does it share the feeding current of the host, thereby gaining an additional supply of nutrients? Are *B. nubilus*'s extremely hooked beaks a morphological adaptation for pruning back and preventing complete overgrowth by encrusting species such as *Halichondria*?

One species garners protection by being associated with the second. The second gains more space on which to live. Is this accidental or has each made reciprocal modifications and sacrifices to further and maintain the partnership?

PLATE 26. *Goose barnacles* Pollicipes polymerus *in outwash*

Although goose barnacles lose in competition with mussels on horizontal surfaces, they apparently thrive on vertical walls, a position conducive to filtering prey from wave run-off rather than wave break.

PLATE 27. *Wave Action*

PLATE 25

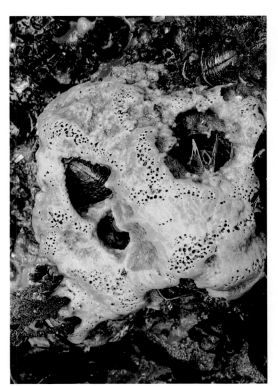

PLATE 26

PLATE 27

CHAPTER THREE

Nature's Variability: Changing Patterns in Time and Space

T HE intertidal zone is in flux from day to day, month to month, and year to year. The variations in time and space that occur at every site may have slight effect or all but drown out the major patterns. On the rocky shores of the temperate zone, the occasional bad storm, the equally devastating spell of cloudless sky and still water that can afflict the intertidal with a desert climate for six hours a day, or even a loose log kicked around by the waves all provide frequent disturbances. Scientists cannot predict when and where these disturbances will occur. Such unpredictable events can kill mussels, limpets, and other animals, and wipe out areas of kelp or other algae, thus providing opportunities for new settlers.

Some of these variations, or "disruptions," are as predictable as the onset of winter. Every year, following the autumnal equinox, storms rip out sea palms and strip many other kelps of their fronds, so that a rocky shore, like a deciduous forest, appears to be a relatively lifeless place in midwinter. Such rhythms are individual: each shore has its own, governed by the seasonal cycles of activity in its long-lived species and the seasonal timing of settlement, growth, reproduction, and death in its shorter-lived members. Some organisms, characterized by their hit-and-run behavior, seem attuned to take advantage of the opportunities opened by these seasonal disruptions. In midwinter, for example, the spores of *Porphyra* settle high on the shore splashed by the same winter storms that defoliate the rocks lower down. As spring comes and the water begins to warm, the defoliated areas of the shore often acquire a slimy coating of diatoms before kelps grow new fronds and crowd out the diatoms with increased shade. None of these opportunists can persist, despite temporary periods when they may blanket the intertidal, because they are poor competitors and/or good to eat.

Different sets of "opportunistic" species characterize the fall and winter. Although seasonality is their hallmark, they usually produce little change in the longer term nature or the appearance of the baseline community. The easiest way to recognize them, and the only way without more precise biological information, is to visit a favorite site a number of times throughout the year and note the pulses of life.

Other disturbances are less predictable: landslides, tornadoes, and forest fires are obvious terrestrial examples. Equally, on land, deep footprints in soft mud, the dirt mounds of moles and badgers, or small erosional gullies are disturbances. In the intertidal, a winter storm can open a gap in a mussel bed, or a winter freeze can kill large expanses of kelp, even whole populations of certain organisms. These events all remove organisms of one sort and in so doing either recycle some limiting resource or present a new resource favoring another and different assemblage.

Biologists are now beginning to understand that disturbance provides an important opportunity for diversity. Too much disturbance can became a monotonous stress with monotonous results, but a moderate frequency enlivens and enriches the environment by creating a "mosaic" made from patches of different ages and sizes.

The character of the biological assemblage within the patches themselves changes with time. This phenomenon of change is generally referred to as *succession*—the pattern of species replacements following some large-scale disruptive event. A landslide-cleared forest, for instance, would be recolonized by a series of plants, each slower to arrive and longer-lived than the last until (usually, but not always) the vegetation in that clearing was restored to its original composition. The same is generally true on rocky shores, except that the colonists are both plant and animal. It is now known that the order in which the species arrive and the nature of their interreactions have the capacity to produce local variations in the replacement sequence. Thus, some of the early views on succession have been called into question. No one would disagree that the species composition of a site changes with time, especially following a major disturbance. At issue are the ecological mechanisms underlying the changing pattern and their generality.

On rocky shores we can identify two prevalent categories of physically caused natural disturbance, both leading to mortality and therefore to change. The first includes both extreme physical and mechanical stresses, as in the destruction of mussel beds by wave action or battering by logs. Individual survival is mediated not so much by superior attributes as by the good fortune of being out of the way when the disruption occurs. This type of disturbance can produce a patchy, heterogeneous population or even a collage of different species, and can be a major determinant in the overall pattern and character of the assemblage.

It is relatively easy to recognize this type of disturbance: gaps in mussel beds, recently overturned boulders, sand scour marks on pier pilings or rocks, or sheets of rock that have exfoliated from the surface. None of these is likely to have been caused by the normal activities of organisms and all are readily related to localized physical stresses.

The second source of mortality is more predictable than the first, and occurs when the physiological limits of an organism are exceeded, for instance, by heat, cold, or insufficient oxygen. These stresses usually come to bear upon organisms at the extremes of their vertical range, most commonly towards the upper limit, and often result in a uniform pattern or band paralleling the water level over a broad geographic area. When a sharp boundary occurs at a population's upper limit, especially when some "opponent" species isn't apparent, the edge suggests that they extend to the limit of their physiological tolerance. Careful observation can often reveal dead or moribund individuals above this limit, especially after periods of extreme heat or cold. Sharp boundaries, however, may also be created by the activities of predators or competitors.

It is important to recognize the distinction between the natural physical disturbances and stresses with which organisms have evolved for eons, and the newer, different stresses introduced by humans that can influence natural communities adversely. Intertidal organisms have obviously adapted to some types of natural physical disturbance, but they may well suffer from additional human-induced stresses. Because opportunistic or "weedy" organisms are apt to mature within a year or less, they are in a sense preadapted to an existence filled with vagaries. The individuals of many species, on the other hand, take more than a year to mature sexually and may attain great age. These individuals cannot respond rapidly to environmental change. Once such species have been removed, they take a while to return: giant sequoia trees recover more slowly from harvesting than dandelions.

Learning to recognize physical disturbance and interpret its traits, some of which are illustrated in the accompanying photographs, provides insights vital for the understanding of our limited rocky shore-lines and their management. Visit, for example, an unpolluted, unexploited rocky shore that is exposed to moderate to heavy wave action. Evidence of small-scale disturbance will be widely present, even stark. The community will be rich in species, many of which are relatively large and long-lived, and much patterning will be visible. At less exposed sites the same assemblage is apt to be simpler: fewer species will coexist and spatial patterning will be less obvious. Finally, examine a polluted or heavily exploited shore. It is a safe bet that this will be weed-dominated, and the longer-lived components absent. Under a normal regime of disturbance, weeds enrich rocky shores. Where people have accelerated the natural disturbance pace through overexploitation or have poisoned the longer-lived, more susceptible species, the community is much less rich.

45

PLATE 28. *Sea Palm*

The sea palm, *Postelsia palmaeformis*, plate 19, has long been recognized as an indicator of persistent and violent wave action. Its occurrence in the middle to high intertidal zone and its unique morphology and graceful resilience when swept by the rapidly moving water have contributed to its renown.

Postelsia depends on disruptive events to clear space for it to occupy. Unlike other disturbance-dependent opportunists, however, *Postelsia* is a good competitor and a poor disperser, confined to a particular and geographically limited habitat. The spatial scale of *Postelsia*'s competitive abilities is approximately the size of the plant's holdfast, which can overgrow mussels and barnacles, usually smothering them in the process. In the early autumn, increasingly heavy wave action yanks some *Postelsia* away, taking the underlying animals (as well as associated plants) with them, and leaving behind a small patch of bare rock into which adjacent *Postelsia* can drip their spores. These small patches in mussel beds probably serve to catalyze further disruption of the surrounding areas, thus making more prime habitat for *Postelsia*.

PLATE 29. *Tidepool with Starfish and Sea Anemone*

PLATE 30. *Sand Abrasion*

Abrasive forces make life especially difficult on emergent rocks surrounded by beach sand. Waterborne particles sandblast the rocks, smoothing and molding them into beautiful shapes. Such sandblasting may bury and kill adult organisms and scour recently settled juveniles from the rock surface. Plate 30 of intertidal rocks at Duk Pt., Washington, was photographed during late winter. In the spring and summer, when the sea is calmer and sand scour less extreme, seaweeds may occupy this habitat.

PLATE 28

PLATE 29

PLATE 30

PLATES 31A & 31B. *Gap in Mussel Bed*

Physical disturbance is particularly conspicuous when it affects species such as the mussel *Mytilus californianus*. Because it is competitively superior, *Mytilus californianus* is able to form expansive beds, or monocultures. Plate 31a shows a mussel bed with two gaps where mussels were swept away. One gap is new (foreground), where the rock is mostly bare except for remnants of byssal threads and large old barnacles, *Semibalanus cariosus*, which had survived beneath the mussels for an unknown period of time. The adjacent gap is older, having formed during the previous winter, and is now thoroughly saturated with small *Semibalanus cariosus* and assorted algae. Plate 31b shows another mussel bed, similarly disrupted. Although the gap now contains a distinctive set of organisms, predominantly the benthic green algae, *Ulva* sp., and some of the red algae *Halosaccion glandiforme*, it also will eventually revert to mussels.

Scientists are as uncertain of why some patches are initially small and others large as they are of the exact mechanisms of patch formation. Predators, floating logs, or the lifting and shearing forces of large waves could all initiate such patches. Once cleared, the patches may continue to grow as wave action further unravels the edges of the surrounding mussel bed. Eventually, however, they are closed, either as mussels encroach inwards from the perimeter or, if the gap is very large, by the settlement of new mussels. Natural disturbances provide space where other organisms can grow during the time it takes the mussels to return, and in many instances this valuable spatial resource is snapped up on a first come, first served basis. The time of the year the gap was opened, its height in the intertidal zone, and its size when formed all affect the further characteristics of the patch, its recolonization, and the subsequent succession of organisms that occupy it.

48

Many rocky shores are characterized by a series of horizontal bands, each dominated by a different conspicuous species of plant or animal and separated from the others by more or less sharp boundaries. The delineations are sharper in some places than others, and this can tell us something important about the local conditions of life. One may find from two to as many as eight clear bands, depending in part on the exposure of the site to wave action.

The photograph in plate 32b, taken on the relatively protected south side of an islet known as Seal Rock just east of Neah Bay, Washington in 1981, shows a zonation pattern almost identical to that in a photograph taken by zoologists at the same place between 1933 and 1938. Like the striking zonation pattern on many mountainsides, this characteristic of the intertidal can remain constant over many years.

The south side of Seal Rock shows four distinct zones: at the top, in the splash zone, a dark band of blue-green algae persists on vertical portions of the rock; next to this in the upper intertidal is a whitish band of the barnacle *Balanus glandula*; beneath this is a wide zone of the mussel *Mytilus californianus*, some appearing white because of the barnacles encrusting their shells; and, last, the lower intertidal is dominated by kelps, principally *Hedophyllum sessile*.

In plate 32a, one can see the slightly more complex zonation pattern than that of Seal Rock characteristic of more exposed habitats. At the top is a dark band of blue-green algae, which is followed sequentially by a band of the barnacle *Balanus glandula*, a fringe of the smaller blue mussel *Mytilus edulis*, a narrow band of the larger blue mussel *M. californianus*, a mixed band of the goose barnacle *Pollicipes polymerus* and the acorn barnacle *Semibalanus cariosus*, followed by a zone inhabited by laminarian algae and a great variety of lower intertidal organisms such as sponges, tunicates, and sea urchins.

Many phenomena, both biotic and abiotic, influence these zonation patterns, and it takes both clever experiment and long-term observation to discover the causes at a given site. Nevertheless, the ubiquity of such striking patterns has made the study of zonation a unifying theme in marine ecology.

PLATE 33A. *Tidepool 1980*
PLATE 33B. *Tidepool 1981*

Plates 33a and 33b, of the floor of the same lower intertidal pool, were taken one year apart. A quick glance at the color difference is enough to reveal the dynamic nature of these assemblages. Some species have been partly eaten, others have moved in or left completely, and others have changed position slightly. The sea anemones are long-lived and although capable of relocating themselves, they don't seem to have moved. The red sponge, *Ophlitaspongia* sp., has persisted in almost the same place, whereas another sessile sponge, the yellow *Mycale* sp., has disappeared; perhaps it was eaten or died of old age. In the second picture two mobile consumers, the small six-armed starfish, *Leptasterias hexactis*, and the keyhole limpet, *Diodora aspera*, are on the scene. *Diodora*, which eats sponges, may have eaten the *Mycale*.

Most intertidal landscapes are so complex, and the changes so subtle, that "time lapse" photography at intervals of months to a year or more is essential if the dynamics are to be recorded adequately.

52

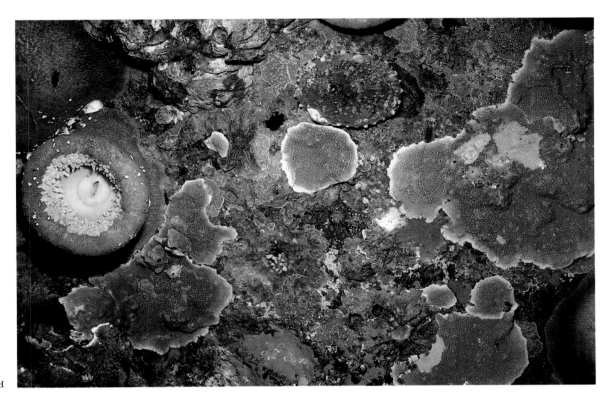

PLATE 33B

PLATE 33A

CHAPTER FOUR

〜〜〜〜〜〜〜〜〜〜〜〜

Predation

ALONG the Pacific coast of North America, predator-prey interactions appear to be of particular consequence to the structure of intertidal communities. Predation governs the distribution of many intertidal organisms, and suggests that their colors, shapes, and behaviors may be understood in terms of the urgent need to avoid being eaten.

Predation is the eating or preying upon of one plant or animal by other animals. This process commonly and effectively removes individuals from the substratum, thereby creating space or other resources for different species. Sometimes, though, the prey is only nibbled or partially consumed, and many marine organisms survive these encounters, eventually regenerating lost parts. In the intertidal one can see some predators seeking or eating their prey, but the activities of others are usually revealed only by bite marks, grazing trails, or the virtual absence of prey species from areas where their predators normally roam.

Consumers are grouped by their characteristic food choices into three generalized categories called *trophic levels:* herbivore, carnivore, or omnivore, depending on whether the food is plant, animal, or both. All three groups ultimately depend on the food energy fixed during photosynthesis by plants, or producers. When we examine the feeding relationships within a whole community, we find a natural hierarchical order in the predation process. To describe this, ecologists have developed the concept of food webs, in which plants are consumed by herbivores which in turn are consumed by carnivores. This more abstract, less observable ecological framework is necessary to describe the resulting flow of energy through a community, but it does not explain the ecological influences of a particular species. Further, predator-prey relationships are thought to be fundamental to understanding the stability or persistence of natural communities, an aspect of major significance as human beings gradually alter most communities, including those on the shore.

Predators often play dramatic and important roles in communities, although the visual evidence of their effects occurs on a less grand scale than some forms of disturbance. For instance, a predator might reduce the numbers of an effective competitor, such as mussels that are capable of dominating an area. The liberated resource can then be invaded by the marine equivalents of weeds, species which require disruption of the status quo and occupy the space only temporarily. Other, more mobile predator species are essentially nomadic, moving from opportunity to opportunity. This dynamic suggests the counterintuitive conclusion that moderately disturbed communities may be the most diverse, since freedom from physical or biological disruption yields ecological monotony. For this reason, perhaps, intertidal communities along exposed shorelines are among the more diverse known.

Predation, and to a lesser extent physical disturbance, are fundamentally involved in explanations of the fabric of nature. Of the three methods of scientific inquiry discussed in the introduction, observation and experimentation have yielded rich data on predation. Some species are absent or rare in what seems to be acceptable habitat. The observed presence of a highly effective predator may explain why. Experiments have demonstrated that local community configuration can change rapidly following quite subtle shifts in the consumer popula- tion. Such demonstrations have enormous implications for applied ecology and the management of our seashore resources, since they show that certain species have an importance out of proportion to their local abundance.

Predation is a conspicuous event and often leaves striking evidence of its occurrence. Many animals are active feeders only during high tide, at other times retreating under rocks, into crevices, or among dense algae where they remain inactive. However, receding tides often reveal natural acts of predation in process, especially when it takes the predator more than one tidal cycle to consume the prey. Subtler forms of ecological evidence may also be present: grazing trails, drilled holes, or chipped shells, to name a few. Their presence provides irrefutable evidence that some consumer passed that way, nibbling, browsing, destroying. Finally, the design features of intertidal organisms become especially noteworthy in the context of predation. Morphological traits such as shell thickness in mussels, the structure of barnacle plates, or even the shape of limpets all suggest adaptations to minimize the chance that they will be eaten. They reflect the continuing contest between predator and prey, with the goal being the avoidance of ex- tinction.

It is possible to interpret behavioral and chemical prey defenses, which include poisonous secretions, noxious taste, pinching, biting, and color, as means evolved to frustrate the efforts of predators. In addition, ecologists think that vulnerable species, or species suscepti- ble to being consumed, increase their survival chances by being highly seasonal or by showing up in unpredictable places, thus escaping in time or space. Conversely, less tangible predator attributes such as long-range chemosensory abilities, acute eyesight, and swiftness have all evolved to enhance an organism's ability to exploit some resource. Although this evolutionary game of hide and seek is ubiquitous, there are excellent reasons for believing that such features serve a variety of purposes. The ribbing on a massive shell, for example, could make the animal more immune to drilling, or could prevent it from being dislodged by wave action. The following pages illustrate many such observable aspects of the predation process, a process that is a vital part of the cycling and turnover of resources within the intertidal zone and that generates fascinating ecological complexities.

PLATE 3 4 . *Wave action*

PLATE 35. *Fish Ambush*

Predators have different tactics for obtaining prey. Some are slow and creeping in their attack, others chase. Some sit and wait but have to conceal themselves while they lie in ambush, since their prey would recognize and avoid them if possible. In plate 35 the smooth-head sculpin, *Artedius lateralis*, common in tidepools and shallow waters, has ambushed a prey item, *Jordania zanope*, a juvenile long-fin sculpin.

PLATE 36. *Sea Anemone Predation*

The sea anemone, *Anthopleura xanthogrammica*, waits for the waves to bring it food or for prey to wander fortuitously within reach, as was probably the case with the crab, *Oedignathus* sp., in plate 36. Many crabs disappear down anemone gullets and are later strewn out as bits of shell after strong enzymes have digested the body parts. These anemones derive the majority of their diet from food swept to them by the waves, particularly uprooted mussels that may have been loosened by foraging gulls or starfish before the waves knocked them free. Thus, anemones are among the major beneficiaries of disruptive wave action, catching these morsels as they fall out of eddying water and moving them to their mouths with tentacles. The ring of tentacles surrounding the mouth is packed with nematocysts, minute stinging structures with microscopic barbs, which are used for defense and food capture. As wave action diminishes, so does the average body size and abundance of *A. xanthogrammica*. This is why one finds them living in places of maximum water flow, often carpeting the bottom of surge channels.

PLATE 35

PLATE 36

PLATE 37. *By-the-Wind-Sailor* Velella velella

These animals are pelagic, floating at the surface in offshore waters. They are at the mercy of winds and are often cast ashore in large numbers. Such large food items washed ashore can be important in the diet of sessile intertidal organisms such as the sea anemone *Anthopleura elegantissima.*

PLATE 37

PLATES 38A, 38B, 38C. *Periwinkle Snails*

Plate 38a shows a cluster of the snail *Littorina planaxis*, which feeds by scraping algae and fine detritus from the rocks. An interesting by-product of their feeding activities is that they remove particles of rock as well; grain by grain they are capable of deepening tidepools by 1 centimeter every sixteen years. In general, animals that feed by rasping and scraping can wear away rock at a rate equal to that of other erosive processes such as exfoliation, chemical solution, or physical abrasion, and when the population is abundant, the erosion resulting from its feeding activities is appreciable.

The small herbivorous snail *Littorina sitkana* grazes on the alga *Enteromorpha* sp. (plate 38b). Many species, including these, are called generalists: they have broad feeding habits and eat a wide variety of prey without showing marked preferences. Others are specialists: they feed on a single or few prey. In plate 38c, an aggregation of *Littorina sitkana* is feeding communally on a detached frond of *Nereocystis* brought within their reach by waves. A single snail probably couldn't anchor the drifting mass, but groups can. This leads one to consider the many possible functions of a snail's shell: to protect the animal from predators, rolling rocks, and desiccation, and to aid in anchoring drifting kelp.

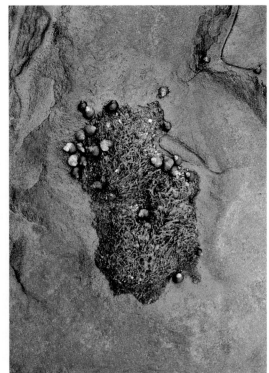

PLATE 39. *Starfish Predation*

The common starfish, *Pisaster ochraceus*, sits characteristically humped up over a prey item, the mussel *Mytilus californianus*, in plate 39. The starfish's preferred prey is mussels but it is a generalist, feeding on barnacles, chitons, goose barnacles, and limpets by spreading over and inserting a part of its stomach into the prey. Once the prey is subdued it is lifted or yanked from the surface and tightly applied against the starfish's oral surface, where it may be almost totally enveloped in the stomach's folds.

The foraging behavior of *Pisaster* involves a vertical movement: the animals move upwards during high tide, capture prey, and often return to a lower tidepool or surge-channel refuge to digest it. The upper limit of their effective foraging is conspicuously marked by a browse line, setting the lower limit to mussel and barnacle populations.

The sea anemones, *Anthopleura xanthogrammica*, are often found near mussel beds, in effect waiting in the wings for a meal generated in part by *Pisaster*'s feeding activities. The anemones, in fact, settled in the mussel bed as larvae and later worked their way downwards, flourishing from proximity and association with the starfish.

One sees *Pisaster* in a variety of colors ranging from ochre or orange through various shades of purple. No reasons for this are known. Gulls that hunt visually are probably not involved, since this species cannot be considered camouflaged or cryptically colored. For whatever reasons, the orange morph is more common along exposed shores and the purple morph is more abundant in calmer, more inland waters.

This starfish has been referred to as a *keystone species*, because it exerts a strong and disproportionate influence on the community structure through its feeding activities, preferentially consuming a prey that could otherwise dominate the space. Like wave-generated physical disturbance, predation restrains or removes one species, making possible an increase in the diversity of others.

PLATE 41. *Limpet and Coralline Algae*

Plate 41 illustrates evidence of grazing on a pink coralline crust, where a species that tends to feed selectively on this resource, the limpet *Acmaea mitra*, has practically grazed it down to bedrock. The lined chiton, *Tonicella lineata* (plate 84, page 125), also feeds on coralline algae; however, very few other animals graze on these rocklike red algae, which are characterized by tissues enmeshed in a matrix of calcium carbonate. The scraping organ, or radula, of these grazing species is considerably harder than that of many other grazers and functions as a combination rasp and conveyor belt. Ecologically, the radula may be suited to a very specific kind of food, thus restricting what the grazer can eat.

Many *Acmaea mitra*, unlike other limpets, are encrusted with coralline algae such as *Pseudolithophyllum whidbeyense*, which in plate 41 is reproductive (the small white dots in the coralline algae on the limpet's back are reproductive structures). Intertidal ecologists have found that a higher proportion of reproductive crusts are found on the backs of limpets than on the rock substratum. Although the encrustation may serve to camouflage the limpet, it is also possible that the safest place for the coralline crust to be is riding piggyback on one of its major consumers.

PLATE 42A. *Sea Urchin Grazing Marks*
PLATE 42B. *Sea Urchins*
PLATE 42C. *Sea Urchin Dominated Seascape*

The sea urchins *Strongylocentrotus purpuratus* exert a tremendous influence on the diversity and abundance of intertidal flora: they can turn a garden of kelp into a pavement of pink crustose coralline algae.

The aggregation of sea urchins in plate 42c almost totally controls the character of the plant community. The herd pictured is in a traditional spot for sea urchins and has been there for at least fifteen years. As their population expands, the sea urchins will fan out, chopping down kelps as they go. In the meantime they collect diatoms and fleshy algae, which they deliver to their mouth parts with their tube feet.

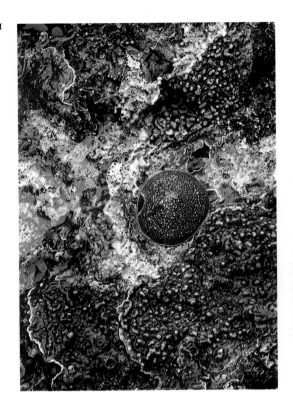

Sea urchins feed while immersed, using an apparatus known as Aristotle's lantern, which is equipped with intricate and efficient jaws for nibbling and scraping food, and perhaps for excavating burrows. Plate 42a shows the star-spangled bite marks of a sea urchin on a piece of kelp.

One can see subtler effects of grazing by *S. purpuratus* in plate 42b, where the halo around each sea urchin came about as it fed on the surrounding black diatomaceous coating. The black chiton, *Katharina tunicata*, has also grazed away a patch of these diatoms. The sea urchins produced the depressions in which they are sitting by scraping with their teeth and perhaps their spines.

One can argue that sea urchin grazing activities are advantageous to the understory coralline algae, for the urchins protect the algae from being overgrown by diatoms or fleshy plants. Algal crusts are always colorful and serve as an excellent indicator of intense grazing pressure at all latitudes. In fact, the predominance of coralline algae in many tropical communities is an accepted hallmark of herbivorous fish activity.

Sea urchins play a major role in the organization of subtidal as well as intertidal communities. Factors influencing their activities vitally affect the benthic algal community. Thus, the presence of sea otters, which eat sea urchins, can make possible lush forests of kelp that urchins would otherwise decimate. The removal of sea urchins, whether by otters in California and the Aleutians or by people and the sunflower starfish, *Pycnopodia helianthoides*, in Washington and Alaska, always produces dramatic changes in the species pool.

PLATE 43 . *Shore Crab*

In plate 43, the lined shore crab, *Pachygrapsus crassipes*, forages by night and hides by day in cracks, in crevices, or under rocks to avoid predation by such diurnal predators as sea gulls and crows. This behavior, known as refuging behavior, is increasingly recognized as an important component in maintaining a balance in the continual warfare between predator and prey. Structurally simple habitats, then, tend to be characterized by fewer species than those with complex topography, which, among other things, provide more hiding places.

PLATE 44 . *Keyhole Limpet*

Rather than running away from starfish, as many limpets do, the common keyhole limpet, *Diodora aspera*, frustrates the efforts of its predators by responding effectively to their proximity or contact. The limpet raises itself off the substrate, extending part of its mantle over its shell and another part downward. This leaves no ready place where the starfish can fasten its tube feet, increasing the probability that the limpet will escape.

PLATE 43

PLATE 44

PLATES 45 & 46. *Plant Chemical Defense*

Antipredator defenses are well documented in terrestrial plants, and include tannins in the leaves of oaks, the poison of poison ivy, and digitalis in foxglove. The brown alga, *Desmarestia* sp., produces sulphuric acid in small cavities, which leak when the alga is damaged. Plate 45 shows *Desmarestia* lying atop other algae; plate 46 shows the bleaching effect the sulphuric acid has had on the underlying plants. The living plant is eaten by few invertebrates, but it isn't known whether the sulphuric acid functions in defense against predators or in competition for space with other organisms, particularly plants. It probably serves both ends, deterring grazing and giving the algae a competitive edge.

PLATE 47. *Nudibranch and Hydroid*

Nudibranchs such as *Coryphella trilineata* usually feed on hydroids—for example, *Eudendrium* sp., as in plate 47. Amphipods sitting on hydroids have been observed attacking and successfully repelling climbing nudibranchs, in the process protecting the hydroid from one of its major consumers. Three-party interactions such as this are challenging to interpret: Are they merely a coincidence or is there substantive biological meaning to them? The amphipod might be protecting its habitat from destruction. If so, it would benefit hydroids to somehow attract amphipods. In nature's open market, where protection, housing, and feeding are exchangeable commodities, "barters" between species are an established practice and can lead to mutual benefit.

PLATE 48. *Limpet Grazing Trail*

In plate 48, a tell-tale grazing trail has been produced in a diatomaceous mat as a grazing limpet rasped its way back and forth. Limpets, littorines, and chitons all influence the microflora, and with practice it is possible to distinguish the feeding marks of these major groups. Although it may appear detrimental, the grazing of certain species is important, because the diatoms or other small algae can foul their surface. Also, if sporelings survive to become larger algae, as they grow they can outcompete the species on which they initially settled.

PLATE 45

PLATE 46

PLATE 47

PLATE 48

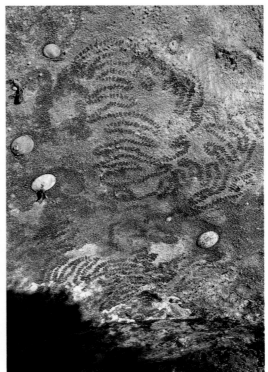

CHAPTER FIVE

ᴧᴧᴧᴧᴧᴧᴧᴧᴧᴧ

Reproduction and Settlement on the Shore

REPRODUCTION is of obvious importance if species are to replace their dead, increase in numbers, or extend their geographical distribution, and it occurs by a startling variety of methods. Natural selection favors the traits of those organisms whose offspring survive to become reproductive, which explains the interest of ecologists in all phases of reproductive biology. Not surprisingly, it is more than just the number of offspring produced by a female that renders her the fittest. One must consider the health and vigor of the offspring and thus their probability of surviving to reproduce, since they will be the bearers of her genes. With birds, it has been shown that in harsh years individuals producing fewer eggs are favored over those attempting to raise larger families. The moral is that fewer is sometimes better, and the logic applies clearly to avian clutch sizes ranging from one egg every other year to about twenty per year. For those marine species in which the clutch size is limited and/or parental care such as brooding is involved, the same constraints against increasingly large clutch sizes probably apply.

When thousands or even millions of eggs are produced, as in many marine organisms, another type of reasoning is required, since reducing the "clutch" from, for example, one million fifteen to one million is not apt to make much difference, or even be measurable. Many species producing large numbers of larvae have great adult longevity and highly variable recruitment success. This combination ensures that occasionally the repopulation process will be successful: it might be called a boom-or-bust strategy. Another characteristic reproductive pattern involves those species whose individuals only reproduce once and then die. In these, natural selection favors the genetic traits of the individuals producing the most offspring.

Reproduction includes two major modes: *asexual*, as in budding, transverse fission, or fragmentation, in which no recombination of genetic material takes place; and *sexual*, in which gametes from two individuals unite to produce a third. In many marine organisms fertilization is external, taking place in the sea, with free-living larvae being produced from the vast numbers of sperm and egg that are shed. Many worms and echinoderms, such as our common sea urchin, fall into this category. In others, fertilization occurs internally within the parent, which then releases larvae into the sea. Barnacles are a familiar example. These life-history patterns are referred to as *indirect development*, since the larvae spend varying intervals of time floating or wandering as plankton in the surface layers of the water before settling to the bottom and adopting adult habits. Other animals lack a free-living larval stage and encapsulate or brood their eggs. A juvenile emerges after metamorphosis and simply crawls away over the rock surface. The snail *Thais* and the brooding starfish *Leptasterias* reproduce in this fashion. This mode of reproduction, in which a miniature replica of the parent is produced, is known as *direct development*.

Interestingly, some species combine these possibilities and reap the varying advantages of both modes. For example, the sea anemone *Anthopleura elegantissima* produces large clones of genetically identical individuals by asexual reproduction; however, some also release sperm or eggs which when fertilized produce larvae genetically different from both parents and capable of dispersing over a wide distance.

For most marine algae and invertebrates, the primary dispersal stage is spores or larvae, morphologically different from their parent and carried unknown distances by water currents. Algal spores probably settle out haphazardly, but the location of newly metamorphosed juvenile invertebrates is based on decisions made by the larva, so marine ecologists have been interested in a quartet of closely related phenomena: larval development and dispersal, habitat selection, and metamorphosis. The phenomenon of dispersal is universal: it amounts to not putting all one's eggs in a single basket and is therefore a strong hedge against local extinction. A species that spreads itself over a larger landscape not only may encounter suitable, unoccupied habitat, but will be much less susceptible to local catastrophes.

The movement of an individual from one location to another, the distance and means of transportation and locomotion, and the life-history stage involved differ markedly among taxonomic groups. There are three benefits to planktonic dispersal: wider genetic exchange, the potential colonization of distant geographic areas, and the ability to take advantage of available habitat. It is very difficult for biologists to trace or identify a particular group of larvae drifting at large in the sea, because the plankton can't be marked and are patchy, making them hard to sample. Consequently, many mysteries remain in this critical process. What is the specific site or population from which particular larvae were derived? How far can the larvae travel? How far are they transported by complex coastal currents? How long can they remain in the plankton, delaying metamorphosis if necessary until an appropriate settlement site is found? When reproduction is indirect, the recolonization of intertidal habitats depends on how well the larvae survive the hazards of the planktonic interval. One can't help but marvel that any survive to adulthood, given the many obstacles. One of the challenges of marine biologists' work is to ascertain from the adult distribution whether its positioning was determined by selective settlement, with the larvae exercising a genuine choice, by the chance survival of recruiting larvae, or both.

Larvae have organs for swimming and attachment, and sense organs to prospect for and identify their habitat. Some larvae react to light, gravity, specific chemical substances, or changes in pressure. They swim or drift until sensory cues tell them to settle. When a mobile larva either voluntarily settles, randomly settles, or is enticed to settle on a spot, the process is referred to as settlement, or *recruitment*. Recruitment is often accompanied by *metamorphosis*, a set of radical changes in the organism's habitat and appearance.

The period spent in landing on a suitable place to live and undergoing metamorphosis preliminary to initiating the postlarval life is critical. Many of the necessary recruitment or settlement decisions are surprisingly specific. Larvae have some freedom and capacity to recognize and distinguish among different habitats, and therefore they exercise some choice. They may settle in proximity to their own kind, in crevices of a given darkness, in water currents of a given velocity, or with another species with which they have a biotic relationship of some type.

The precise mechanisms by which larvae test, explore, and crawl about surfaces are not well known, but the fact that some can attach temporarily, or can delay metamorphosis and spend long times in the plankton, suggests that marine animals, unlike dandelion or maple seeds, do not settle at random. Once metamorphosis has been initiated, it is usually completed in a remarkably short time, and immediately afterwards the settled juvenile is faced with a new suite of predators and competitors. The relationship between adults and juveniles can take many forms, with the highly vulnerable juvenile stage being protected in some instances and left to its own devices in others.

Settling larvae may discriminate between surfaces. For instance, they prefer certain kinds of rock over others for a variety of reasons: the rock's texture, the presence of an appropriate surface film, or the extent of conditioning by chemical bleaching. Some living surfaces defend themselves from would-be settlers by mechanical devices or chemical means. For instance, some echinoderms, including starfish, have pedicellaria—pinching structures useful for protecting their surfaces. Some of the benthic algae may be too smooth; others may secrete noxious chemicals to inhibit settlers.

Reproduction superbly illustrates many trade-offs and ecological compromises. Small eggs, for example, are metabolically cheaper to manufacture than larger ones, and therefore can be produced in proportionately larger numbers. An egg mass brooded by a parent or laid in a capsule uses more energy, yet is more secure from the vagaries of life than an embryo free-floating in the open sea, but this benefit is bought at the sacrifice of dispersal. Furthermore, the brooding adult may be committed to an interval of voluntary starvation. One can identify similar problems facing reproductive adults: for instance, an individual that spawns early in the year may increase the probability that its offspring will have first access to optimal settlement sites, but the larvae may encounter unfavorable environmental conditions. Additionally, what may be a secure spawning location for the adults may be a hostile site for the larvae.

Considering the enormous variation in reproduction, it is impossible not to wonder about the relative advantages of particular strategies. What are the offsetting advantages of sexual versus asexual reproduction, of the sexes being separate or the individual being a true functional hermaphrodite? What is it about the production of egg capsules that might outweigh the advantages of long-distance dispersal? If animals broadcast gametes and fertilization takes place externally in the sea, how often does one find individuals successfully repopulating the shore? With some groups, such as limpets and barnacles, one often finds juveniles; in others, such as starfish and sea urchins, the presence of juveniles is much less predictable. These variations and a great many more questions of basic significance continue to intrigue biologists.

PLATES 49A & 49B. *Intertidal Algae*

The life history of benthic marine algae is highly complex, offering to the unsuspecting biologist a maze filled with pitfalls and riddles. Essentially it involves the alternation of a sexual and an asexual generation within each species, although in some the alternate phase is either unknown or bypassed. In some cases these algal generations are iden-

tical morphologically; such species are referred to as *isomorphic*. In other species—called *heteromorphic*—one generation looks entirely different from its counterpart. The latter situation is challenging to phycologists, because if the plant cannot be cultured in the laboratory there is no guaranteed way to associate the two phases with one another. Plates 49a and 49b show *Mastocarpus (Gigartina) papillata* and *Petrocelis middendorffii*, respectively, the two phases in the life cycle of a single red alga. Morphologically they are distinctive; they are also very different ecologically. *Petrocelis*, the encrusting asexual form, is perennial and very long lived, apparently attaining ages over 90 years. *Mastocarpus*, the textured upright blade form, reproduces sexually and is thought to be an annual.

Complexities such as these can have profound economic importance. Many red algae have been traditional fare for maritime cultures. Of commercially exploited red algae, *Porphyra* is the most familiar and a food item (*nori*) treasured by the Japanese. *Porphyra* culture now supports a $2 billion a year industry, but sustained economic yield was not possible until the microscopic alternative phase, *Conchocelis*, was found living subtidally within calcareous rock and clam shells.

PLATE 50. *Intertidal flora, including the bright red algae,* Erythrophyllum delesseroides, *which are found in places of low light intensity such as tidepools nestled below overhanging rocks.*

PLATE 50

PLATE 51. *Sea Grass and Seed-bearing Shoots*

The marine benthic flora is well represented by lower plants: large algae, some fungi, benthic diatoms, and blue-green algae. It also includes the so-called sea grasses, which are most closely allied to the taxonomically more advanced terrestrial plants and actually produce flowers and seeds. *Phyllospadix scouleri* is a perennial sea grass that occurs on wave-swept shores and is attached to rocks or wedged in crevices by means of its creeping rhizomes and roots. This plant has the capacity to swamp out entire tidepools, although, as in mussels, the tendency is thwarted by wave action or other forms of disturbance. *Phyllospadix* produces a shoot bearing seeds (plate 51); pollination occurs underwater with the help of water currents. *Zostera*, another sea grass, occurs in more protected habitats. Both these plants are important as nursery grounds for economically important fish and crustaceans. When they detach, they are also a major source of organic debris and contribute this material, known as detritus, to distant food webs. *Zostera* rhizomes help stabilize the sediment, and the blades are a vital food source for migrating waterfowl such as brant.

PLATE 52. *The Blood Star* Henricia *sp.*

PLATE 53. *Coralline Algae and Their Reproductive Structures*

In the crustose coralline alga *Pseudolithophyllum muricatum* (plate 53) the reproductive structures are visible as a field of small white dots. These are called *conceptacles*, fertile cavities opening to the surface of the plant. Marine coralline algae are isomorphic, meaning that the two alternating generations look alike. The positioning of the conceptacles, whether raised or sunken, is thought to be related to the influence of grazing pressure over evolutionary time. Specific structural variations can discourage herbivores and minimize browsing; the plant may be erect or encrusting and thin or relatively thick, and varying amounts of calcium carbonate may be deposited in its walls. In the tropics, where grazing pressure is even heavier than along the temperate Pacific coast, one can find calcareous brown and green algae as well as red.

PLATE 5 1

PLATE 5 2

PLATE 5 3

PLATE 5 4 A . *Bull Kelp*
PLATE 5 4 B . *Beached Kelp*

Nereocystis luetkeana is an abundant species of kelp. The conspicuous phase of this annual plant (plate 54a) is one of the largest of brown algae, attaining lengths in excess of 15 meters. It is capable of growing as much as 6 centimeters a day. When the plant matures, vast numbers of swimming spores are produced and liberated. These become a cohort of bottom-dwelling microscopic plants, which then reproduce sexually, yielding in the next generation the massive *Nereocystis* phase that forms great forests just off shore. Towards the ends of their lives, the large plants often become entangled, detaching themselves and each other from the rock. The holdfast in marine plants only anchors the plant to the bottom; unlike the roots of most land plants, it does not take up nutrients or water. Therefore, once torn loose, the plants are still capable of reproduction and growth, as long as they continue to be exposed to water circulation and light. As wrack cast up on the shore, they provide food and habitat for many small organisms (see plate 54b).

PLATE 5 5 A . *Nudibranchs Mating*
PLATE 5 5 B . *Nudibranchs and Egg Ribbons*
PLATE 5 5 C . *Egg Ribbon on Hydroid Stalk*

Encounters between two individuals of the nudibranch *Hermissenda crassicornis* (plate 55a) can be aggressive, but more often they occur for purposes of mating. These organisms are hermaphrodites, capable of both making and fertilizing eggs. The mating pair cross-fertilizes each other, and then each lays its eggs encased in capsules formed into a soft gelatinous string, distinctively looped. Egg masses vary from species to species but are often highly individualistic and may contain from a few to a million eggs. Eventually they disintegrate and the larvae hatch and swim away. Plate 55b shows the wide egg ribbon of the nudibranch *Archidoris montereyensis*, and in plate 55c the narrow coil of eggs of another nudibranch is attached to a hydroid stalk.

One risk of this life style is potential cannibalism. Many opisthobranchs, including *Hermissenda*, are generalized feeders that become reproductive at a relatively small size and engage in rituals that involve mouthing or biting one another. This may result in one of the two being eaten, particularly if it is much smaller. In this way some individuals of the population will indeed be better fed, and it serves as an effective means of population control.

PLATE 56A. *Wave-carved Seascape, Tatoosh Island, Washington, nest site of many marine birds. Gulls are probably the most important predator of the goose barnacles* Pollicipes polymerus. *Other marine birds are known to consume large numbers of limpets, mussels, littorines, and sea urchins.*

PLATE 56B. *Snail Broadcasting Eggs*

In plate 56b, the snail *Calliostoma ligatum* (with a highly eroded shell) is releasing eggs. This is the most common mode of reproduction for intertidal invertebrates. The eggs are broadcast in the sea, where fertilization takes place. The fertilized eggs develop into a larval stage which drifts an unknown time and distance before settlement. Life for planktonic larvae is very hazardous: the longer the time spent in the plankton, the greater are the chances of the larvae dying before settlement. On the other hand, an extended planktonic interval increases the possibilities of traveling longer distances and encountering higher quality habitat. Herein lies a very subtle balance between risk and reward.

PLATE 57A. *Anemone Asexual Reproduction*
PLATE 57B. *Anemones Shedding Sperm*

The sea anemone *Anthopleura elegantissima* is capable of two modes of reproduction, sexual and asexual. In plate 57a it is seen reproducing asexually by longitudinal fission, a process that takes about two days to complete. To some extent it appears that fission is stimulated by starvation; a hungry anemone, by dividing, tends to increase the size of its mouth relative to its metabolic needs. In plate 57b, sperm are being shed into the water, while individuals elsewhere shed ova. Fertilization takes place in the water when these meet. The species is hedging its bets in an ecological and evolutionary sense. Fission permits a genotype (clone) to occupy or monopolize space rapidly, potentially excluding invaders. Sexual reproduction is favored for dispersal to new habitats in addition to maintaining genetic variability, an important way of adjusting to an unpredictable and changing world.

PLATE 58. *Brooding Sea Anemone*

Epiactis prolifera, the sea anemone in plate 58, maintains a sex life unique among animal species. Its young, which are brooded around its base, are not formed by budding but are produced sexually. Eggs of the female parent are fertilized by planktonic sperm in her digestive cavity, where the embryos develop into motile larvae. They then escape through her mouth, glide down and become embedded in the column, where they remain until they are fully formed and ready to migrate away. They begin to migrate when they are three months old and five millimeters high.

In this limited dispersal strategy, life must be better closer to home for the young *Epiactis*. Yet somehow they have persisted, colonizing intertidal zones from Alaska to Southern California. If you assume that they originated at the southern end and walked north, fifteen hundred miles seems a long distance to go, even in the fifteen thousand years since the retreat of the last coastal glaciers. For this reason, ecologists often consider alternative mechanisms, for instance hitchhiking on debris such as the holdfasts of uprooted and drifting kelp or sea grass.

The small six-armed starfish *Leptasterias hexactis* (plate 82, page 123) also broods its young. Mature individuals are thought to congregate, with both sexes spawning more or less simultaneously. As the female liberates eggs, she collects into a cluster those that don't slip away, holding them with her tube feet and arching over them for six to eight weeks until the juvenile sea stars, 1.5–2 millimeters in diameter, are released. During that time, the brooding female cleans the egg mass, and because the position of the eggs blocks her mouth, she does not feed. While brooding, *Leptasterias* is more susceptible to being knocked off the substrate by waves because it holds on only with the tips of its arms. In rough water, it must allocate more of its tube feet to hanging onto the rock than in calm waters, decreasing the available brood area. In this way the rigors of the environment directly affect reproductive

PLATE 58

output. With no planktonic dispersal stage, what accounts for the great geographic range of this species? It is found along the Pacific coast from Washington to California and is abundant on the Cobb Seamount, which lies offshore, 270 miles west of Washington State. Perhaps it is rafted from site to site by uprooted drifting kelp, such as *Nereocystis*, on which it sometimes crawls.

PLATES 59A & 59B. *Snails and Egg Capsules*

Mature individuals of the largely subtidal snail *Ceratostoma foliatum* sometimes gather in clusters in the intertidal to reproduce. After mating, females deposit eggs in fluted yellow teardrop capsules (plate 59a), which are attached to each other and to the rock. An adult female produces approximately forty egg capsules a year, each containing thirty to eighty eggs. Embryonic development, including metamorphosis, occurs within the capsule, and a miniaturized snail emerges in about four months.

The snail *Thais canaliculata* breeds in spring and summer. After mating, the female deposits eggs in teardroplike capsules 6–11 mm high, in clusters attached to the rocks in shaded situations (plate 59b). This species is one of several in which more eggs are laid in each egg capsule than actually develop; those that do not develop, called nurse eggs, are later eaten by the developing larvae to supplement their food supply.

PLATE 60. *Sea Palm, Mussels, and Barnacles*

The marine plant *Postelsia palmaeformis* (plate 60) characterizes and has been used as an indicator of the exposed wave-swept rocky shores of western North America. *Postelsia* inhabits high-wave-energy environments, particularly on vertical walls where disturbance is virtually guaranteed, and is conspicuous because of its palm shape and moderate size (half a meter tall). Its mode of reproduction gives *Postelsia*, like *Epiactis* and *Leptasterias*, very limited dispersal abilities, and the offspring are unlikely to be far from the parent. Like many other marine plants, it releases huge numbers of spores, but they colonize primarily only within 3 meters or less of the parent plant. During sporulation, which occurs at low tide and while the plant is being splashed, the spores drip down the plant's grooved blades onto the rock below. This species is an annual, completing both phases of its life cycle within a year and dying after reproduction. Thus it is in its "invisible" phase during winter, but becomes increasingly conspicuous through growth, from each spring on. Like other plants with gas-filled floats, or fronds, *Postelsia* has the capacity to float great distances; however, the efficiency of this mode of colonization must be relatively low, since it depends on a fertile plant being cast ashore and releasing spores on a suitable site. Since *Postelsia*'s propagules don't commonly disperse very far, exploitation of it, whether for food or as a source of algal sugars, is certain to lead to local extinction unless great care is exercised. This danger clearly highlights the adaptive significance of dispersal. The question remains, however: why is *Postelsia* so committed to a local strategy?

PLATE 61. *Calcareous tube worm,* Serpula vermicularis, *with its feathery feeding apparatus extended for filtering food.*

PLATE 62. *A lower intertidal surge channel with sea urchins and sea anemones under a canopy of the kelp* Laminaria setchellii.

98

PLATE 60

PLATE 61

PLATE 62

PLATE 63. *Barnacle Settlement*

Barnacles are representative of a large number of invertebrate species whose larvae spend two to three or more weeks in the plankton. These larvae, loaded with sensory devices, can closely discriminate and identify the substrate on which they are settling. The larvae of the small barnacles in plate 63 have already made their choice, settled, and in the process of metamorphosis, shed much of their larval equipment. Now, attached to the substrate, they have assumed the appearance of miniaturized adults. Note that the distribution of these small, brown *Chthamalus dalli* appears to be related to the texture of the rock on which they settled. Many of them occur in tiny cracks, suggesting that this microenvironment is especially favorable to survival. The biological question is whether they choose to settle in such places or whether their current distribution reflects more general settlement with higher survival in the little cracks and furrows. A major source of barnacle mortality is limpets which as they move around dislodge small, recently metamorphosed barnacles. This phenomenon is referred to as bulldozing and affects small balanoid barnacles more than it does *Chthamalus*. Thus, one might expect balanoid barnacles to choose sites without limpets in which to settle and, in general, for early survivorship of all barnacles to be enhanced by textured surfaces.

Larval capacities for habitat discrimination are important, for the choice, once made, commits the individual to a particular spot for life. Individuals that make inappropriate choices are not apt to survive to reproduce, which explains the need for such sophisticated abilities during the critical transition from planktonic to benthic life.

PLATE 64. *Top Shells* Calliostoma ligatum

PLATE 63

PLATE 64

PLATE 65 . *Sea Urchin Recruitment*

Sea urchins are typical of a great many marine invertebrates: the adult is abundant and its ecology well known while the early life-history events just after metamorphosis are almost unknown. Many urchins prefer to settle close to adults, where presumably they are protected under a canopy of calcareous spines. It is known that urchins can live a long time, and in many areas recruitment to the population by larvae is irregular, with large numbers of young recruiting only once or twice a decade. This unpredictable pattern underscores the many dangers of human exploitation. Not only is the adult reproductive stock being removed, but so is the source of settlement cues or protection for the larvae. Under these circumstances, the rate of recovery after exploitation has ceased is apt to be slowed. In plate 65, a juvenile *Strongylocentrotus purpuratus*, probably one to two years old, has emerged from under the canopy of an adult sea urchin. This is a species in which size is not a good indicator of age, for individuals are capable of increasing and decreasing in size in response to environmental conditions. Size, however, does indicate reproductive capacity in this case, as larger individuals have more gonad and can leave more offspring.

PLATE 65

PLATE 66. *Mating Crabs*

Plate 66 shows two crabs, *Cancer productus*, mating, an activity that involves the male grasping and carrying the female around for several days before she molts, after which the eggs are fertilized. The male will remain with his mate until after her new shell has hardened enough for normal activity. The female carries the developing young under her abdomen, protecting them for some time. Eventually the eggs hatch and the larvae escape to become members of the plankton.

PLATE 67. *Aggregation of starfish* Pisaster ochraceus *and the brown alga* Hedophyllum sessile.

PLATE 66

PLATE 67

CHAPTER SIX

The Role of Color

Bright colors contribute much of the magic of the intertidal, and their possible meanings are intriguing. Pigments may be obtained through diet or manufactured metabolically, and their use by individuals in recognition, camouflage, or to warn off potential predators suggests an adaptive function. Frequently, though, the biological significance of these brilliant hues remains a mystery.

Light, particularly solar radiation, is the fundamental source of energy for the life-giving process of photosynthesis, and without light there would be no color. The watery environment itself changes some of the properties of light and vision as we know them. Because light is absorbed and scattered as it penetrates water, underwater vision can be compared to that on land in fog. Beyond a certain depth the only light that remains is that of bioluminescent origin, light produced by the organisms themselves from photophores or bacteria. It is in the uppermost zones of the marine environment, then, that brilliant colors, subtle hues, varied patterns, warning coloration, and camouflage are best developed. In addition, the extravagant use of color characteristic of the ocean's lighted zones implies relatively good vision, as is true for some crabs and octopus, and there are birds and fish whose color vision is comparable to ours, which is the standard against which all others are compared.

Color vision is only postulated for a few marine invertebrates, and color discrimination has been demonstrated for still fewer. In one such experiment the hermit crab, *Pagurus*, was shown to discriminate between painted yellow and blue snail shells and shells colored different shades of grey. Most other intertidal species at least have photoreceptors of one sort or another that can identify differences in light intensity, but we don't know whether such organisms detect color or movement, whether they can form an image, and, if they can, how they respond to such stimuli. And, even though the octopus eye is capable of forming an image, its visual perception must be different from ours. It is often difficult enough to understand what imagery lies in the mind of a human "beholder"; the problems are greatly magnified when marine invertebrates are under consideration.

Many colors have no known biological significance. In some organisms they are the result of deep colored tissue showing through other, more transparent body parts; in other animals brightly colored organs remain concealed within opaque bodies or shells; and many vividly colored animals live in burrows from which they rarely emerge. With both the level of visual acuity and the ability to detect color in question for most intertidal organisms, the role of color has been difficult to ascertain.

Color is of enormous significance to organisms that are eaten by predators relying on visual cues to locate and capture prey. Consequently, many of the examples of adaptive coloration illustrated here could also have been considered in the chapter on predation, particularly as examples of prey defenses. As such, color is usually not an interactive process among organisms themselves, but rather the result of one such as predation.

To interpret the significance of color requires a broad understanding of an organism's life style. For some animals there may be a protective advantage in being as conspicuous as possible, perhaps to advertise some unpalatable or noxious quality. One wonders if the predators of invertebrates learn to associate color with certain unpleasant attributes, such as inedibility or high risk, as has been well documented for birds. Color may also help one individual recognize another of its own species and to choose mates; it is just possible that the varied hues and patterns of hermit crabs may be used in this fashion.

From our viewpoint the enormous range of marine plant colors is enigmatic. They all possess the green pigment chlorophyll essential for absorbing light used in photosynthesis; however, they may derive their color from a mix of photosynthetic pigments, the proportions of which determine the color we see. Sometimes masking or accessory pigments are present in sufficient quantity to disguise the pigment determining the division to which the plant belongs. Thus, some high intertidal red algae (division Rhodophyta) appear brown.

Organisms that blend into and are often indistinguishable from their backgrounds are said to be *cryptic*. Crypsis may originate from behavior, genetic factors, or developmental processes, and requires the ability to select a matching background. It assumes a seeing eye capable of color vision from which to hide. Other animals employ mimicry, essentially fooling the predator by resembling some other more distasteful or dangerous form.

Some animals, including some abalones and top shells, gain their color as a result of diet, perhaps because pigments in their food aren't metabolized and are somehow transferred and laid down in their bodies or shells. Although this procedure may seem rather casual, it guarantees that an organism, eating what's around it, will inadvertently and generally match its background coloration. Many animals have color both fixed and beyond their control, but some of these also belong to a species that is polymorphic, existing in a number of color modes. Some animals acquire protective color passively or actively on their exterior surfaces, such as the deceiving collections that decorator crabs take up on their carapaces. Others are capable of modifying their color by use of chromatophores, pigment-containing cells that can be manipulated by the animal's musculature to produce color change in a flash.

When an organism stands out against its background, are we seeing a technique for self-advertising or has it wandered into foreign and potentially hostile habitat? What is the function of the bright and highly characteristic nudibranch colors? Why should the large barnacle *Balanus nubilus* have a sulphur-yellow mantle? Why should hydrocorals stuffed under rocks be purple, orange, or red? And why should sponge and starfish exhibit the colors they do? Many uses of color are represented in the photographs that follow, but examples also appear of intertidal color that we cannot explain with certainty regarding cause or functional significance. Thus, it is color—on both dainty and grotesque species found under rocks or in caves both high and low in the intertidal zone—with its pronounced influence on human visual sensations, that continues to intrigue biologists and many others, who wonder whether nature's striking and ornate displays are simply capricious or signify important biological interrelationships.

PLATE 68. *The Sunflower Starfish* Pycnopodia helianthoides

PLATE 69. *Iridescent Algae*

There are three groups of large benthic algae: reds, browns, and greens. Some of the red algae are iridescent: their color changes as one's angle of view does—a delightful phenomenon and one distinct from the biochemical production of colors from pigments. The phenomenon may have different causes in different algae. In *Iridaea cordata*, plate 69, iridescence is produced on the blade of the plant by an outer *cuticle*, a series of thin, laminated layers of cells spaced in such a way that the structure internally absorbs one wavelength of the spectrum's rays while reflecting the rest. This pattern produces contrasting indices of refraction, or iridescence. Oddly enough, the color of these plants may be incidental to one of the cuticle's functions—that is, protecting the plant's tissues from attacks by grazing amphipods.

PLATE 70. *Red Algal Crust* Hildenbrandia *sp.*

PLATE 71. *Intertidal Flora*

The saclike plant *Halosaccion glandiforme* (a red alga), shown in plate 71, can vary in color from yellow to dark red as the amount and color of the light striking the plant vary. In addition, some of the variation may be induced by the plant's reproductive state. Also seen are a green alga, *Ulva* sp., and both crustose and erect forms of coralline algae, which are reds.

In addition to illustrating variations in plant color, the plate hints at the range of morphological variety so characteristic of algae. *Ulva* is essentially a two-layered sheet of photosynthetic tissue. The sheet form presents a large surface area to the sun, thus maximizing photosynthetic area with minimal strain on the holdfast, and is the commonest form in the intertidal. The adaptive significance of the *Halosaccion* form, a balloon of tissue surrounding a cavity partially filled with sea water, has not been investigated. Perhaps the entrapped water helps keep the plant moist and cool by evaporative water loss when exposed

PLATE 69

PLATE 70

PLATE 71

III

on a hot day. Or—again, perhaps—the internal water holds the plant off the surface and makes it more difficult for herbivores to eat.

The coralline algae all start out as discs closely adherent to the rock surface. Some never depart from this life form and, although showing wide variation in thickness, surface texture, and positioning of the reproductive structures, remain and are referred to as crustose coralline algae. The other corallines begin as a crustose basal system that eventually develops erect branches composed of many-jointed plates. The erect forms are as varied and taxonomically difficult as the crusts.

PLATE 72 . *Intertidal Algae*

Plate 72 illustrates a number of species of algae. Particularly conspicuous is a species of brown algae, *Pelvetia* sp. Its characteristic color comes from an accessory photosynthetic pigment that both protects the primary pigments and contributes to the plant's productivity. The moss-like *Cladophora* sp., a green alga, is also present.

PLATE 73 . *A small sea anemone* Tealia *sp. and mobile organisms: a crab, the snail* Calliostoma ligatum, *sea urchin* Strongylocentrotus droebachiensis, *and the chiton* Katharina tunicata.

PLATE 72

PLATE 73

113

PLATE 74. *Detail of lower intertidal marine alga,* Desmarestia *sp.*

114

PLATE 74

115

PLATE 75. *The floor of a surge channel with sea anemones and sponge. (Note that all of the rock surface is inhabited.)*

PLATE 76. *Brittle Star*

Ophiopholus aculeata (plate 76) is another echinoderm, a brittle star, that exhibits extremely varied hues and patterns for no known reason. The variations of the arms are independent of the design of the central disc, and no two *Ophiopholus* have been found to be exactly alike.

116

PLATE 75

PLATE 76

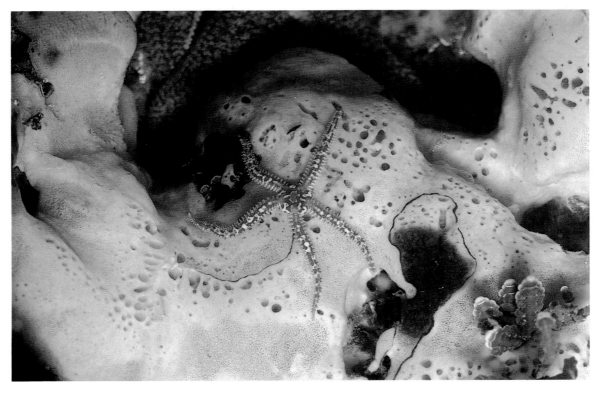

PLATE 77 . *Nudibranch*

Individual members of a species may exhibit a high degree of variation in color and pattern owing to a combination of genetic factors, the arrangement of pigments, or variations in diet. This is certainly true of *Hermissenda crassicornis*, plate 77; however, this nudibranch is always recognizable, even in juvenile stages, by the presence of a brilliant orange stripe down its back and bright blue lines along each side. In general, nudibranchs may be either cryptic or conspicuously colored. Nudibranchs such as *Hermissenda* do have something noxious to advertise. Their diet is composed largely of coelenterates such as hydroids that possess nematocysts, minute stinging structures. These are swallowed whole, transported through the gut and across its lining unexploded, and eventually lodge in club-shaped or branching dorsal protuberances called ceratae, where they serve to defend the nudibranch. Some species wave their ceratae when disturbed. This striking bright coloration of the nudibranch is thought to be a warning to predators not to eat them. How effectively it works and whether the predators learn to associate the nudibranch's color and pattern with inedibility isn't known.

PLATE 78 . *Starfish* Pisaster ochraceus *near the low water mark.*

PLATE 77

PLATE 78

PLATE 79. *Nudibranch*

In plate 79, the nudibranch *Diaulula sandiegensis* is easy to spot. Its hard, gritty texture may contribute to discouraging predators, as might the prominent ring-shaped markings on its back, the number of which varies from individual to individual. For an organism without vision, such as this, the color displayed in ring shapes may possibly function in two ways. Like the false eyes on fish and birds, the rings might appear to be a large eye and startle predators. Or the "eye" might simply serve to break up an otherwise continuous surface color, thereby rendering the nudibranch more cryptic. If nudibranchs had excellent color vision we would have to consider another hypothesis—that the striking colors serve as sexual signals to prospective mates.

PLATE 80. *Cryptic Isopod*

Color and form together often make an animal difficult to detect or follow, as in the isopod *Idotea* sp., in the center of plate 80. The isopod's exoskeleton, which is composed of overlapping plates, is well suited to blend with the articulated architecture of erect coralline algae. When the animal and plant share a common coloration, the crypsis is near perfect. One problem with this strategy is that the isopods are restricted to coralline algal turf, since when they leave it they become conspicuous prey items.

Another and less common form of protective coloration occurs when one animal species assumes the body form and coloration of another in order to gain protection. Such mimicry usually involves imitation of well-defended, aggressive, or inedible species.

PLATE 81. *Nudibranch, Egg Masses, and Sponge*

The nudibranch *Rostanga pulchra* and its egg masses are usually found on one of its preferred prey items, the red sponge *Ophlitaspongia pennata*. As the nudibranch feeds it incorporates pigments from the sponge. The eggs it lays in a transparent jelly matrix are also brightly colored, but as development proceeds they become paler.

PLATE 79

PLATE 80

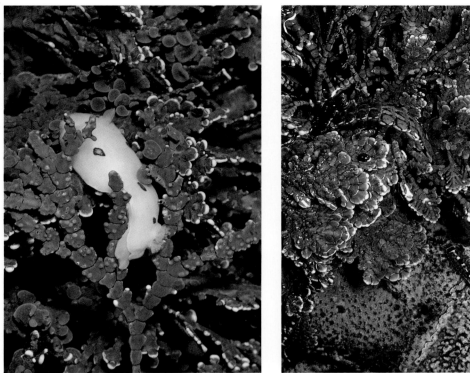

PLATE 81

PLATE 8 2 . *Six-Armed Starfish*

The small six-armed starfish *Leptasterias* is color polymorphic. Individuals within the species exist in a wide range of colors, including brown, green, white, yellow, pink, and nearly black, one of which is seen in plate 82. Color polymorphism in this species is believed to be genetic, little influenced by diet or age. Predators that hunt visually—crabs, birds, and fish—may selectively remove the starfish most easily spotted and leave behind the ones on matching substrate.

PLATE 8 3 . *The blood star,* Henricia *sp., perched atop two of its food items, the sponge* Halichondria panicea *and bryozoan* Cryptosula *sp.*

PLATE 82

PLATE 83

123

PLATE 8 4 . *Lined Chiton*

In plate 84 is the small lined chiton *Tonicella lineata*, whose markings, sinuous or zigzag lines, resemble those of no other Pacific coast species. In contrast to *Leptasterias*, the color of *Tonicella* is known to be modified by diet. They are pinker when eating coralline algae and greenish when feasting on diatoms.

PLATES 8 5 A & 8 5 B . *Cryptic Coloration in Fish*

Oligocottus maculosus, a small sculpin, is expert at matching its background, such as the rock in plate 85a. This species is abundant on rocky shores, especially in tidepools. Another sculpin, *Clinocottus* sp., also demonstrates the ability to match its background, a sponge, in plate 85b. Animals such as octopus and the fishes can rapidly alter their color in relation to background color and light intensity by use of chromatophores, and they know when they have reached a good match. Such controlled use of color makes their predator's search more difficult. On the other hand, it may serve to conceal the fish, as predator, from its prey.

PLATE 84

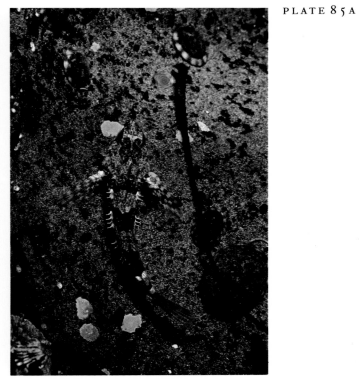

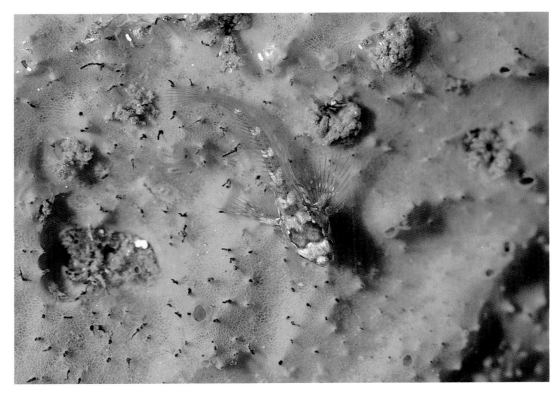

PLATE 86. *Goose Barnacles* Pollicipes polymerus

PLATE 86

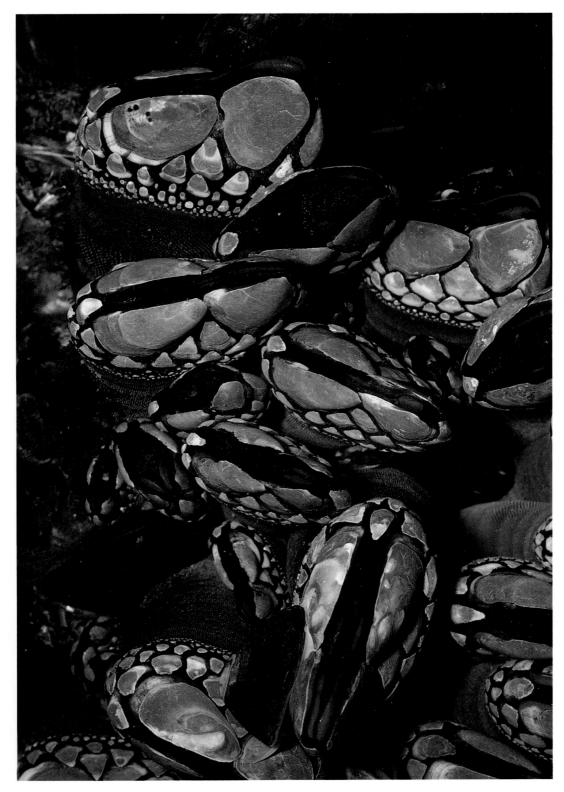

PLATE 87. *Decorator Crab*

An interesting camouflage technique is seen in certain crabs. The crab exoskeleton is an armor composed of nonliving tissue; therefore the adjustable color patterns characteristic of fish and octopus aren't possible for these species. Crustaceans have used at least two techniques to counter this limitation. In the first, small-bodied crustaceans will match their background coloration. The second solution is seen in larger bodied species, which are bound to have greater food requirements and therefore must move around more. These are unlikely to be adapted to some local color. This solution is illustrated by the spider crab, *Oregonia gracilis*, which decorates itself with a veritable garden and/or bestiary on its back. *Oregonia*, as pictured in plate 87, is covered with a luxuriant growth of tunicates and sponges. This camouflage is actively acquired, transplanted, and maintained by the crab and must be replaced after each molt. It produces a generalized coloration, texture, and outline well suited to the crab's general feeding and habitat requirements. The rough texture of *Oregonia*'s carapace encourages settlement of various colonists, but the crab also has delicate pinchers on its first pair of legs that are well designed for handling and planting bits and pieces of plant and animal decoration. Other species become camouflaged passively and acquire an epibiota naturally, as in the limpet *Acmaea mitra* (plate 41, page 69). Such uncontrollable growth can also be detrimental, making organisms more susceptible to being dislodged, as witnessed in many limpets, mussels, chitons, and even large algae found stranded along the beach after storms.

PLATE 88. *Solitary Corals*

Balanophyllia elegans (plate 88) is the only true coral occurring intertidally along the Pacific coast. It is most often found under ledges, in caves, and in other dark places. The bright polyp is retractable into a stony craterlike skeleton with its radiating ridges, which appears bony and chalk white when the animal dies. Currently, there is no explanation for the distinctive color of this coral.

PLATE 87

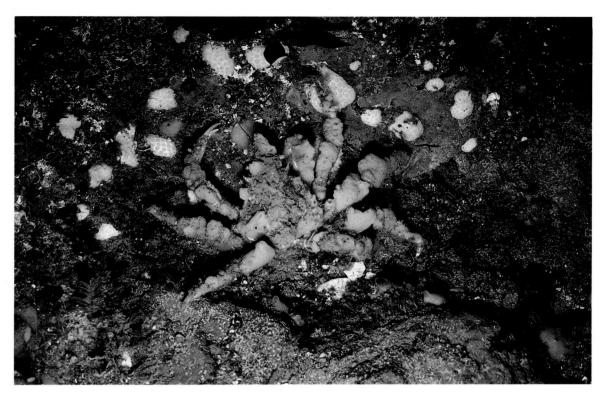

PLATE 88

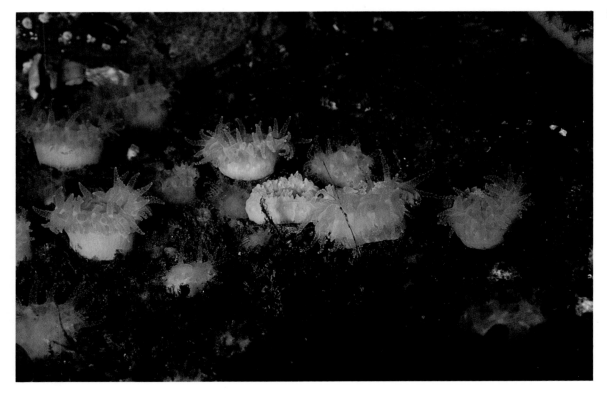

PLATE 89. *Sea Anemones*

The color of the sea anemone *Anthopleura xanthogrammica* (plate 89) can be attributed in part to natural pigmentation, but mainly to symbiotic green algae. The two types of algae that can live within the anemone's tissue are zoochlorellae and zooxanthellae. One or both of them become concentrated in the tissue lining the digestive tract, branches of which extend into the core of each tentacle. The value of the association is in part a nutritional one; organic compounds produced by the plants are utilized by the anemone. The algal endosymbionts use the anemone's carbon dioxide (CO_2) and nitrogenous wastes in photosynthesis. *A. xanthogrammica* is more fit with the algae than without, yet in areas of low light intensity where photosynthesis isn't possible, the anemone survives without the symbiont and is much paler in color.

PLATE 90. *Starfish Color*

The vividly colored starfish *Orthasterias koehleri* (plate 90) is found very low in the intertidal zone. It ranges from pink to bright red with markings in a variety of other colors. In general, starfish coloration remains a little-understood phenomenon. Many species are brightly colored and many of these have no known noxious qualities other than pedicellaria, or pinching organelles. Starfish vision, at best, is confined to a few photoreceptors at the tips of the arms. Hence, their lovely colors are a scientific puzzle.

PLATE 89

PLATE 90

Appendix

TIDE TABLES

TIDE TABLES for the west coast of North America are available in the newspaper, at boat marinas and fishing supply stores, or directly from the National Oceanic and Atmospheric Administration (U.S. Department of Commerce). These tables give daily predictions of the times and heights of high and low water for each day of the year at a number of places, designated as reference stations. Usually tidal differences are given too, from which one can calculate the approximate times and heights of the tide at many other sites (tide tables also contain the times of rise and set for both the sun and the moon). For anyone interested in knowing more about what generates tides, I suggest the explanation offered in Thomas Carefoot's book, *Pacific Seashores* (see the reading list at the end of this book).

Each month there are two series of good low tides, which are associated with the new and full moon. On the Pacific coast, the series with the lowest tides generally occurs during the early to late mornings of the spring and summer. During fall and winter, the low tides occur later in the day and often fall after dark.

San Francisco (Golden Gate Bridge), California May 1984				Aberdeen, Washington May 1984			
Day	*Time*	*Ht./ft.*	*Ht./m.*	*Day*	*Time*	*Ht./ft.*	*Ht./m.*
18	0041	5.8	1.8	18	0241	10.2	3.1
Fri.	0733	−1.0	−0.3	Fri.	0942	−1.5	−0.5
	1520	4.5	1.4		1612	7.9	2.4
	1936	3.2	1.0		2148	3.3	1.0

The accompanying sample tide table is for two North American sites on Friday, May 18, 1984. Here for San Francisco the highest tide, 5.8 feet, occurs at 0041 (12:41 A.M.) and the lowest tide, −1.0 feet, at 0733 (7:33 A.M.), daylight saving time notwithstanding. If you want to know the predictions for Point Reyes, California, look at the listing of tidal differences based on the datum for San Francisco. It will tell you to subtract 26 minutes from the predicted time of low water, making the low tide at 7:07 A.M., and that there is no difference to be applied to the height of low water. For another site the difference might be as much as an hour and a half later than that predicted for San Francisco. Be sure to note these local differences in tide predictions; there's nothing more frustrating than getting to the shore two hours after the tide has turned, only to watch a prime area disappear under the water.

On the west coast of the United States, the tidal height of 0.0 is the mean of the lower of the two low waters of each day. What this means for intertidal-goers is that any tide of 0.0 or slightly lower (indicated by a minus sign) will fleetingly expose all the upper and middle intertidal and some of the lower zones. A −1 foot tide will go out a little farther, and the exceptionally low −2 feet tides will expose even more of the intertidal zone. As a check of the tables will reveal, in the course of a year there may be only two or three dozen of such superb opportunities (low tides of −1.5 to −2.0) to explore the intertidal zone.

SOME THOUGHTS ABOUT SAFETY

Whenever you make an excursion to the intertidal zone, always learn the predicted times and heights for high and low water, keeping in mind that these predictions of sea level can be affected by numerous factors such as wind, swells, and barometric pressure—conditions that can vary dramatically from site to site and day to day.

At any given locale and on any particular tide, it is prudent to study the nature of the water conditions and the lay of the land, and to note where waves are breaking and washing. Certain organisms, by nature of their habitat requirements, will tell you something about specific conditions around you. For instance, the presence of the sea palm, *Postelsia palmaeformis*, indicates that the area is subject to heavy surf. Before actually venturing into the intertidal zone, it is also advisable that you study the area and determine a "safe" spot or an escape route should an unexpectedly large wave roll in. If you are ever caught by an unexpected wave, try not to panic and don't run. Lie down, if possible behind an embankment of some sort, hang on, and let the water rush over you.

While in the intertidal zone keep an ear tuned at all times for significant changes in the ocean's roar. Periodically check your watch and the tidal height so that the rising tide won't strand you by cutting you off from a safe route back to shore.

Wear foot gear that will provide good traction and keep you relatively dry. For comfort's sake, a pair of wool gloves (the fisherman's fingertipless type) will keep you warm and help prevent "barnacle bites"—the endless scrapes and scratches that result from negotiating barnacle-covered rocks. Be prepared to get sprayed occasionally by splash from rogue waves.

Within the limits of common sense, however, don't hesitate to explore. And have a good time!

INTERTIDAL ETIQUETTE

We can partake of the shore's delicate beauty without offending, overpowering, or destroying it, but to respect this habitat we do have to monitor our conduct. Visits to the intertidal zone require great sensitivity to the resident plants and animals.

How can we minimize the adverse effects of looking at organisms, handling them, taking them away to eat, or simply walking about among them? To begin with, just getting around the intertidal poses its share of problems.

Try to step on bare rock when possible, remembering that it can be slippery when covered with a thin film of diatoms or crustose algae. In the middle intertidal zone, where fleshy algae make the surface treacherously slippery, the acorn barnacles and mussels make much better footing. One can hardly avoid walking on them, but do tread as lightly as possible. These easily crushed barnacles are important to the economy of the shore, for they are major prey for a large number of invertebrate predators and they provide settlement sites for algae as well. Even the empty valves serve as refuge sites for small organisms, such as littorines, amphipods, and sundry worms. Walking on mussels may weaken their structural continuity and make them more vulnerable to the shearing forces of waves. In the lowest intertidal, sea urchins that have been trampled often suffer broken spines and must devote energy to repairing the damage rather than to other essentials of urchin life such as growth or reproduction.

Piles of dead or dying organisms stranded above the high water line are often the blatant signs of human disturbance. If you do exercise your curiosity by handling animals, replace them in their natural habitat. Some animals are easily damaged by being picked up. For instance, if you attempt to pry a starfish from the rocks, some of its tubefeet or occasionally an arm may break, increasing the eventuality that the animal will be dislodged or destroyed by wave action. Sea urchins need their tube feet as well, for if their ability to hold onto the rock is diminished, they may be washed into the mouths of large sea anemones.

Even the simple act of replacing certain organisms requires some concern and common sense. Place the starfish in deep tidepools where gulls can't extract them. A haphazard toss of a crab or chiton may result in well-fed anemones. Take care to place the animals upright and on acceptable habitat. This is especially true for limpets and chitons, which cannot right themselves easily and cannot attach to most algae. For them, rock is better.

Nearly all animals are endangered by being removed from where they belong. Use care in turning over rocks to see what lives under them and return the rocks to their original positions afterwards, since the animals you find under such rocks or seaweed are probably there for a reason. Perhaps they can't withstand periods of desiccation, or perhaps by being underneath things they achieve some measure of protection from predators. Don't destroy their habitats.

Copies of state laws governing the harvesting and collecting of marine organisms are available at offices of the Department of Fish and Game. If you are planning to do any collecting, you should familiarize yourself with these regulations and be sure to avoid those areas where collecting is prohibited. If you are considering eating certain shellfish, such as clams or mussels, be sure to check for warnings of paralytic shellfish poisoning. At certain times during the year, organisms such as these concentrate a toxin produced by the plankton they eat, and ingesting "hot" clams or mussels can be fatal for humans.

The harvesting of mussels can accelerate disruption of the mussel bed and will produce habitat alterations just as clearcutting a forest does. Harvesters take only one species purposefully, but may have drastic effects on a wide variety of others. Such examples are reasonably common and suggest a ripple effect of some magnitude, especially when the larger organism being exploited or damaged provides the more specialized habitats required by many others.

Sea urchin gonads are a delicacy to some palates. Urchins, like the starfish *Pisaster ochraceus*, play particularly important roles in the organization of our rocky shores, and substantial reductions in their local abundance produce wide-sweeping changes in the intertidal landscape—for instance, the unrestricted spread of mussels and kelps. Visitors to the shore must be sensitive to these possibilities.

The young of some organisms, such as starfish, sea urchins, and sea anemones, recruit only every few years; others, such as the edible sea palm, whose young almost never grow more than 5 feet from their parents, disperse poorly. Still others, such as the larvae of our largest sea urchin, *Strongylocentrotus franciscanus*, preferentially (and maybe exclusively) are attracted to adult individuals, where they find shelter under a forest of spines. Larvae of our goose barnacle, *Pollicipes polymerus*, sometimes recruit to patches of bare rock, but also to stalks of adult individuals. Organisms such as these, which don't recruit regularly, which recruit to established individuals of their own kind, or which are poor dispersers, will be slow to recover if removed. What would our shores be like without them?

Preservation, however, should include all species regardless of size and regardless of whether they play a particular known role. Thus, while scientific debate rages on the economic and ecological benefits of conservation, a parallel argument could be built on esthetic principles alone. A deep satisfaction comes of seeing, understanding, and caring for the natural world.

ANIMAL PHYLA

In the following synopses I have tried to list a few major features that determine why an animal belongs to a particular phylum and, on occasion, some features useful for distinguishing them in the field. I have omitted animal groups that aren't commonly found in the intertidal zone. At a glance, some groups are very confusing—for example, there are tunicates that look like sponges, erect bryozoa that are difficult to distinguish from hydroids, small limpets that may mimic small barnacles, and a bryozoan that looks like a tunicate. Needless to say, brief summaries like these are fraught with the problems of oversimplification and may not be adequate for making such distinctions. For anyone interested in knowing more about these animals groups, I suggest E. N. Kozloff's book, *Seashore Life of the Northern Pacific Coast*.

ANIMAL DIVISIONS

Phylum Porifera: Sponges. These consist of cells, many not even in definite layers, organized around a system of pores, canals, and chambers through which water is moved. There are no body organs, but the sponge is supported by a skeleton of spicules and fibers. The texture is often feltlike or gritty, and one or more openings from which water currents flow are visible. Sponges may be encrusting or vaselike in form.

Phylum Cnidaria: Jellyfish, Sea Anemones, Hydroids, and Cup Corals. In these the body wall consists of two cellular layers with the gut being the only cavity. There is no anus, and the single opening, the mouth, is surrounded by tentacles. These animals are radially symmetrical—that is, in cross-section they look like a wagon wheel.

Phylum Platyhelminthes: Flatworms. These bodies have three layers of cells and bilateral symmetry. Intertidal members of this group are usually flat and broad. All are carnivorous, and pigmented eye spots are visible in the larger flatworms.

Phylum Nemertea: Ribbon Worms. These are slender, usually slightly flattened, and highly elastic in length. Many are very colorful. They possess a complete digestive tract with a mouth at one end and an anus at the other, as do all the groups discussed from this point on. They also have a circulatory system. A unique feature is their proboscis (an extensile organ), which is used to capture prey. When extruded, it often looks as though another worm is being disgorged.

Phylum Annelida: Segmented Worms. The most characteristic feature is the segmentation of the body, usually with groups of bristles associated with the segments. These worms also have a circulatory system, complete digestive tract, and—a feature not seen in earlier groups—a body cavity, or coelom, a fluid-filled space between the digestive tract and outer body wall.

Phylum Mollusca: Snails, Limpets, Chitons, Squid, Clams, Octopus, and Mussels These animals have an unsegmented body plan divided into head, muscular foot, and visceral mass and covered by a mantle, which in most species secretes a shell and shelters the gills. The shell may be one unit, two hinged together, or eight shells in a row. Their organ systems are well developed and in some, like the octopus, the sensory capacities are extraordinary. Because the molluscan shell fossilizes quite readily the fossil record for this group is rich and extends back over 500 million years.

Phylum Arthropoda: Crabs, Hermit Crabs, Isopods, Amphipods, Acorn Barnacles, Sea Spiders, Goose Barnacles, Shrimp (and Insects and Spiders). This is the largest of all phyla and shows enormous diversity. The animals tend to be divided into well-marked sections often grouped together in functional regions: head, thorax, and abdomen. They have a hard, chitinous exoskeleton and jointed appendages. Sensory organs, especially antennae and eyes, are well developed.

Phylum Bryozoa: Lace or Moss Animals. These animals always live attached to something and have a shingled or imbricated surface. They form colonies in many configurations of essentially separate microscopic individuals with a chitinous or calcareous skeleton. The animals have a lophophore—a U-shaped feeding structure that is a ring of tentacles surrounding the mouth.

Phylum Echinodermata: Starfish, Brittle Stars, Sea Urchins, and Sea Cucumbers These animals are radially symmetrical, often pentamerous (five-rayed) with protruding calcareous skeletal structures, mobile tube feet operated by a water-vascular system, a complex digestive system, and a nervous system.

Phylum Chordata: Tunicates and the Familiar Backboned Types such as Fishes, Birds, Mammals, Reptiles, and Amphibians. These all have a notochord, dorsal nerve cord, and gills or gill slits; however, tunicates have these chordate characteristics in the larval stage only. Most tunicates are sessile, growing singly, in clumps of several individuals, or as colonial masses in various shapes. Each individual has an incurrent and excurrent opening; both are often visible. The texture is usually firm with a slick surface.

PLANT DIVISIONS

It is difficult to trace precisely the origin and evolutionary relationships of the algae. They are classified according to pigmentation, general structure, food-storage products, and reproductive patterns, and the following paragraphs list some major features of the plant divisions represented in the intertidal. All algae use the green pigment—chlorophyll—for photosynthesis. The color of an alga, however, is usually due to accessory pigments that mask the green color.

Division Cyanophyta. These blue-green algae, or cyanobacteria, are inconspicuous but important in marine waters. They are most obvious above the high tide line of cliffs and rock walls in areas where there is some seepage. They are very simple organisms in terms of the structure of their cells (they lack chloroplasts and nuclei) and are believed to be ancestral to all other algae. Their color is variable but they have the blue (phycocyanin) and red (phycoerythrin) pigments.

Division Chlorophyta. Green algae are believed to be the ancestral stock from which land plants were derived. The group consists mostly of one-celled species, long filaments made up of chains of single cells, broad flat sheets, and thick growths composed of many fine filaments woven together. They lack accessory pigments and thus they are usually green in color.

Division Bacillariophyta. Diatoms are one-celled plants that sometimes form filamentous colonies and that may have cell walls composed of silica. They store food as oil droplets within the plants. They occur in vast, uncountable numbers and are eaten by almost everything in the sea either directly or indirectly. They contain brown (phaeophytin) pigment, which gives them a golden brown color.

Division Phaeophyta. Brown algae possess fucoxanthin, a brown pigment. They are morphologically the most varied division: filaments, stalks with blades, hollow sacs, and cushion-shaped, to name a few plant forms. They also contain the largest growing algal groups, the kelps that exceed 300 feet in length. Two unique features of this group are the kelp holdfasts (home for many organisms) and the float bladders, some of which are partly composed of carbon monoxide gas.

Division Rhodophyta. These are the reds with the pigment phycoerythrin and a variety of other pigments. Hence, their colors vary. There are many plant shapes and styles of organization within the phylum: simple or finely branched filaments, broad sheets and crusts with variable texture, toughness, and rigidity. They are the most advanced of the algal groups in terms of their reproductive structures and are notorious for their taxonomic difficulty.

Further Reading

THE FIRST LIST provides references to general books on marine biology and ecology, natural historical details of the intertidal plants and animals, and the taxonomy of Pacific coast organisms. The second list contains more technical books and the scientific literature relevant to the patterns and processes illustrated. These numbered references are followed by a third listing that groups them by plate number. By no means are all these references exhaustive; nor do they necessarily include references to the initial work. Rather, for the reader interested in pursuing these subjects further, they provide documentation of the phenomena discussed and an introduction to the scientific literature.

I

1. Abbott, I. A., and C. J. Hollenberg. *Marine Algae of California*. Stanford, Calif.: Stanford University Press, 1976.

2. Branch, G., and M. Branch. *The Living Shores of Southern Africa*. Cape Town, South Africa: Struik, 1981.

3. Brusca, G. J., and R. C. Brusca. *A Naturalist's Seashore Guide—Common Marine Life of the Northern California Coast and Adjacent Shores*. Eureka, Calif.: Mad River Press, 1978.

4. Carefoot, T. H. *Pacific Seashores: A Guide to Intertidal Ecology*. Vancouver: Douglas; Seattle and London: University of Washington Press, 1977.

5. Hedgpeth, J. W. *Introduction to Seashore Life of the San Francisco Bay Region and the Coast of Northern California* (California Natural History Guides, 9). Berkeley and Los Angeles: University of California Press, 1962.

6. Kozloff, E. N. *Keys to the Marine Invertebrates of Puget Sound, the San Juan Archipelago, and Adjacent Regions*. Seattle and London: University of Washington Press, 1974.

7. Kozloff, E. N. *Seashore Life of the Northern Pacific Coast* (revised edition of *Seashore Life of Puget Sound, the Strait of Georgia, and the San Juan Archipelago*, 1973). Seattle and London: University of Washington Press, 1983.

8. Lewis, J. R. *The Ecology of Rocky Shores*. London: English University Press, 1964.

9. Morris, R. H., D. P. Abbott, and E. C. Haderlie (with 31 text contributors). *Intertidal Invertebrates of California*. Stanford, Calif.: Stanford University Press, 1980.

10. Portmann, A. *Animal Camouflage*. Ann Arbor: University of Michigan Press, 1959.

11. Ricketts, E. W., and J. Calvin. *Between Pacific Tides* (fourth edition, revised by J. W. Hedgpeth). Stanford, Calif.: Stanford University Press, 1968.

12. Smith, R. I., and J. T. Carlton (eds.). *Light's Manual: Intertidal Invertebrates of the Central California Coast* (third edition). Berkeley and Los Angeles: University of California Press, 1975.

13. Stephenson, T. A., and A. Stephenson. *Life Between Tidemarks on Rocky Shores*. San Francisco, Calif.: W. H. Freeman, 1972.

14. Thomson, R. E. *Oceanography of the British Columbia Coast* (Canadian Special Publication of Fisheries and Aquatic Sciences 56). Ottawa, Canada: 1981.

15. Waaland, J. R. *Common Seaweeds of the Pacific Coast*. Seattle: Pacific Search Press, 1977.

II

16. Barnes, H., and E. S. Reese. Feeding in the pedunculate cirriped *Pollicipes polymerus* J. B. Sowerby. *Proc. Zool. Soc. London* (1959) 132: 569–585.

17. Barnes, H., and E. S. Reese. The behavior of the stalked intertidal barnacle *Pollicipes polymerus* J. B. Sowerby with special reference to its ecology and distribution. *Journal of Animal Ecology* (1960) 29: 169–185.

18. Barnes, J. H., and J. J. Gonor. The larval settling response of the lined chiton *Tonicella lineata*. *Marine Biology* (1973) 20: 259–264.

19. Bernstein, B. B., S. C. Schroeter, and K. H. Mann. Sea urchin (*Strongylocentrotus droebachiensis*) aggregating behavior investigated by a subtidal multifactorial experiment. *Canadian Journal of Fisheries and Aquatic Science* (1983) 40(11): 1975–1986.

20. Birkeland, C. Biological observations on Cobb Seamount. *Northwest Science* (1971) 45(3): 193–199.

21. Black, R. The effects of grazing by the limpet *Acmaea insessa* on the kelp *Egregia laevigata* in the intertidal zone. *Ecology* (1976) 57(2): 265–277.

22. Bloom, S. A. The motile escape response of a sessile prey: A sponge-scallop mutualism. *Journal of Experimental Marine Biology and Ecology* (1975) 17: 311–321.

23. Bold, H. C., and M. J. Wynne. *Introduction to the Algae: Structure and Reproduction*. New Jersey: Prentice-Hall, 1978.

24. Castenholz, R. W. The effect of grazing on marine littoral diatom populations. *Ecology* (1961) 42: 783–794.

25. Chadwick, E. M. P. A comparison of growth and abundance for tidal pool fishes in California and British Columbia. *Journal of Fish Biology* (1976) 8: 27–34.

26. Chia, Fu-Shiang. Brooding behavior of a six-rayed starfish *Leptasterias hexactis*. *Biological Bulletin* (1966) 130(3): 304–315.

27. Comfort, A. L. The pigmentation of molluscan shells. *Biological Review* (1951) 26: 285–301.

28. Connell, J. H. The influence of interspecific competition and other factors on the distribution of the barnacle *Chthamalus stellatus*. *Ecology* (1961) 42: 710–723.

29. Connell, J. H. A predator-prey system in the marine intertidal region. 1. *Balanus glandula* and several predatory species of *Thais*. *Ecological Monographs* 40: 49–78.

30. Connell, J. H. Community interactions on marine rocky intertidal shores. *Annual Review of Ecology and Systematics* (1972) 3: 169–192.

31. Cook, E. F. A study of food choices of two opistobranchs, *Rostanga pulchra* MacFarland and *Archidoris montereyensis* Cooperi. *Veliger* (1962) 4: 194–196.

32. Cott, H. B. *Adaptive Coloration in Animals*. London: Methuen, 1940.

33. Crisp, D. J. Factors influencing the settlement of marine invertebrate larvae. In P. T. Grant and A. M. Mackee, eds., *Chemoreception in Marine Organisms*. London and New York: Academic Press, 1974.

34. Dayton, P. K. Competition, disturbance, and community organization: The provision and subsequent utilization of space in a rocky intertidal community. *Ecological Monographs* (1971) 41: 351–389.

35. Dayton, P. K. Two cases of resource partitioning in an intertidal community: Making the right prediction for the wrong reason. *American Naturalist* (1973) 107: 622–670.

36. Dayton, P. K. Dispersion, dispersal, and persistence of the annual intertidal alga *Postelsia palmaeformis* Ruprecht. *Ecology* (1973) 54: 433–438.

37. Denny, M. W., T. L. Daniel, and M. A. R. Koehl. Mechanical limits to size in wave-swept organisms. *Ecological Monographs* (1984), 55: 69–102.

38. Dethier, M. N. Disturbance and recovery in intertidal pools: Maintenance of mosaic patterns. *Ecological Monographs* (1984) 54(1): 98–118.

39. Druehl, L. D., and J. M. Green. Vertical distribution of intertidal seaweeds as related to patterns of submersion and emersion. *Marine Ecology Progress Series* (1982) 9: 163–170.

40. Duggins, D. O. Kelp beds and sea otters: An experimental approach. *Ecology* (1980) 61: 447–453.

41. Dunn, D. F. Reproduction of the externally brooding sea anemone *Epiactis prolifera* Verrill, 1869. *Biological Bulletin* (1975) 148: 199–218.

42. Dunn, D. F. Dynamics of external brooding in the sea anemone *Epiactis prolifera*. *Marine Biology* (1977) 39: 41–47.

43. Ebert, T. A. Growth rates of the sea urchin *Strongylocentrotus purpuratus* related to food availability and spine abrasion. *Ecology* (1968) 49: 1075–1091.

44. Ebert, T. A. Recruitment in echinoderms. In J. Lawrence and M. Jangoux (Eds.), *Echinoderm Studies*. Rotterdam, The Netherlands: Balkema, 1982.

45. Edmunds, M. Protective mechanisms in the Eolidacea (Mollusca Nudibranchia). *Journal of the Linnean Society of London (Zoology)* (1966) 47(308): 27–71.

46. Emson, R. H., and R. J. Faller-Fritsch. An experimental investigation into the effect of crevice availability on abundance and size-structure in a population of *Littorina rudus* (Maton): Gastropoda: Prosobranchia. *Journal of Experimental Marine Biology and Ecology* (1976) 23: 285–297.

47. Eppley, R. W., and C. R. Bovell. Sulphuric Acid in *Desmarestia*. *Biological Bulletin* (1958) 115: 101–106.

48. Estes, J. A., and J. F. Palmisano. Sea otters: Their role in structuring nearshore communities. *Science* (1974) 185: 1058–1060.

49. Estes, J. A., N. S. Smith, and J. F. Palmisano. Sea otter predation and community organization in the western Aleutian Islands, Alaska. *Ecology* (1978) 59: 822–833.

50. Feder, H. M. The food of the starfish *Pisaster ochraceus* along the California coast. *Ecology* (1959) 40: 721–724.

51. Feder, H. M. Growth and predation by the ochre sea star *Pisaster ochraceus* (Brandt), in Monterey Bay, California. *Ophelia* (1970) 8: 161–185.

52. Field, L. H. A description and experimental analysis of batesian mimicry between a marine gastropod and an amphipod. *Pacific Science* (1974) 28(4): 439–447.

53. Fletcher, W. J., and R. W. Day. The distribution of epifauna on *Ecklonia radiata* (C. Agardh), J. Agardh and the effect of disturbance. *Journal of Experimental Marine Biology and Ecology* (1983) 71: 205–220.

54. Forester, A. J. The association between the sponge *Halichondria panicea* (Pallas) and scallop *Chlamys varia* (L.): A commensal-protective mutualism. *Journal of Experimental Marine Biology and Ecology* (1979) 36: 1–10.

55. Francis, L. Intraspecific aggression and its effect on the distribution of *Anthopleura elegantissima* and some related sea anemones. *Biological Bulletin* (1973) 144: 73–92.

56. Francis, L. Social organization within clones of the sea anemone *Anthopleura elegantissima*. *Biological Bulletin* (1976) 150: 361–376.

57. Frank, P. W. Effects of winter feeding on limpets by black oystercatchers, *Haematopus bachmani*. *Ecology* (1982) 63(5): 1352–1362.

58. Futuma, D. J., and M. Slatkin. *Coevolution*. Massachusetts: Sinauer Associates, 1983.

59. Gaines, S. D. Herbivory and between-habitat diversity: The differential effectiveness of a plant defense. *Ecology* (1985), 66: 473–485.

60. Gerrodette, T. Dispersal of the solitary coral *Balanophyllia elegans* by demersal planular larvae. *Ecology* (1981) 62: 611–619.

61. Harger, J. R. Competitive co-existence: Maintenance of interacting associations of the sea mussels *Mytilus edulis* and *Mytilus californianus*. *Veliger* (1972) 14(4): 387–410.

62. Hartwick, E. B. Foraging strategy of the black oystercatcher (*Haematopus bachmani* Audubon). *Canadian Journal of Zoology* (1976) 54: 142–155.

63. Hazlett, B. A. Interspecific negotiations: Mutual gain in exchanges of a limiting resource. *Animal Behavior* (1983) 31: 160–163.

64. Hedgpeth, J. W. The living edge. *Geoscience and Man* (1976) 14: 17–51.

65. Hines, A. H. Reproduction in three species of intertidal barnacles from central California. *Biological Bulletin* (1978) 154: 262–281.

66. Hines, A. H., and J. H. Pearse. Abalones, shells and sea otters: dynamics of prey populations in central California. *Ecology* (1982) 63(5): 1547–1560.

67. Huey, R. B., and P. E. Hertz. Is a jack-of-all-temperatures a master of none? *Evolution* (1984) 32(2): 441–444.

68. Jackson, J. B. C., and L. Buss. Allelopathy and spatial competition among coral reef invertebrates. *Proceedings of the National Academy of Science (USA)* (1975) 72: 5160–5163.

69. Koehl, M. A. R. The interaction of moving water and sessile organisms. *Scientific American* (1982) 247(6): 124–134.

70. Koehl, M. A. R., and S. A. Wainwright. Mechanical adaptations of a giant kelp. *Limnology and Oceanography* (1977) 22(6): 1067–1071.

71. Kohn, A. J. Feeding biology of gastropods. *The Mollusca*, vol. 5; Physiology, Pt. 2. New York and London: Academic Press, 1983.

72. Landenberger, D. E. Studies on selective feeding in the Pacific starfish *Pisaster* in southern California. *Ecology* (1968) 49: 1062–1075.

73. Lang, J. C. Interspecific aggression by scleractinian corals. II. Why the race is not only to the swift. *Bulletin of Marine Science* (1973) 23: 260–279.

74. Leighton, D. L. Observations on the effects of diet on shell coloration in the red abalone *Haliotis rufescens* Swainson. *Veliger* (1961) 4: 29–32.

75. Lindberg, D. R. *Acmaeidae: Gastropoda, Mollusca.* Pacific Grove, Calif.: Boxwood Press, 1981.

76. Lubchenco, J. Plant species diversity in a marine intertidal community: Importance of herbivore food preference and algal competitive abilities. *American Naturalist* (1978) 112(983): 23–39.

77. Lubchenco, J. Algal zonation in the New England rocky intertidal community: An experimental analysis. *Ecology* (1980) 61(2): 333–344.

78. Lubchenco, J., and J. Cubit. Heteromorphic life histories of certain algae as adaptations to variations in herbivory. *Ecology* (1980) 61(3): 676–687.

79. Lubchenco, J., and S. D. Gaines. A unified approach to marine plant-

herbivore interactions. I. Populations and communities. *Annual Review of Ecology and Systematics* (1981) 12: 405–437.

80. Mann, K. H. Seaweeds: Their productivity and strategy for growth. *Science* (1973) 182(4116): 975–981.

81. Margolin, A. S. The mantle response of *Diodora aspera*. *Animal Behavior* (1964) 12: 187–194.

82. Margolin, A. S. A running response of *Acmaea* to seastars. *Ecology* (1964) 45: 191–193.

83. Mauzey, K. P. Feeding behavior and reproductive cycles in *Pisaster ochraceus*. *Biological Bulletin* (1966) 131: 127–144.

84. Menge, B. A. Foraging strategy of a starfish in relation to actual prey availability and environmental predictability. *Ecological Monographs* (1972) 42: 25–50.

85. Menge, B. A. Effect of wave action and competition on brooding and reproductive effort in the seastar *Leptasterias hexactis*. *Ecology* (1974) 55(1): 84–93.

86. Menge, B. A. Brood or broadcast? The adaptive significance of different reproductive strategies in the two intertidal sea stars *Leptasterias hexactis* and *Pisaster ochraceus*. *Marine Biology* (1975) 31: 87–100.

87. Muscatine, L. Experiments on green algae coexistent with zooxanthellae in sea anemones. *Pacific Science* (1971) 25: 13–21.

88. Nicol, E. A. T. The feeding mechanism, formation of the tube, and physiology of digestion in *Sabella pavonina*. *Trans. Roy. Soc.* (Edin.) (1930) 56(23): 537–596.

89. Nicotri, M. E. Grazing effects of four marine intertidal herbivores on the microflora. *Ecology* (1977) 58: 1020–1032.

90. North, W. J. Size distribution, erosive activities and gross metabolic efficiency of the marine intertidal snails *Littorina planaxis* and *L. scutulata*. *Biological Bulletin* (1954) 106: 185–187.

91. Osman, R. W., and J. A. Haugsness. Mutualism among sessile invertebrates: A mediator of competition and predation. *Science* (1981) 211: 846–848.

92. Ostarello, G. L. Natural history of the hydrocoral *Allopora californica* Verill (1866). *Biological Bulletin* (1973) 145: 548–564.

93. Paine, R. T. Food web complexity and species diversity. *American Naturalist* (1966) 100: 65–70.

94. Paine, R. T. A note on trophic complexity and species diversity. *American Naturalist* (1969) 103: 91–93.

95. Paine, R. T. Intertidal community structure: Experimental studies on the relationship between a dominant competitor and its principal predator. *Oecologia* (1974) 15: 93–120.

96. Paine, R. T. Disaster, catastrophe and local persistence of the sea palm *Postelsia palmaeformis. Science* (1979) 205: 685–687.

97. Paine, R. T. Food webs: Linkage, interaction strength and community infrastructure. *Journal of Animal Ecology* (1980) 49: 667–685.

98. Paine, R. T. Ecological determinism in the competition for space. *Ecology* (1984) 65: 1339–1348.

99. Paine, R. T., C. J. Slocum, and D. O. Duggins. Growth and longevity in the crustose red alga *Petrocelis middendorffii. Marine Biology* (1979) 51: 185–192.

100. Paine, R. T., and S. A. Levin. Intertidal landscapes: Disturbance and the dynamics of pattern. *Ecological Monographs* (1981) 51(2): 145–178.

101. Paine, R. T., and R. L. Vadas. The effects of grazing by sea urchins, *Strongylocentrotus* sp., on benthic algal populations. *Limnology and Oceanography* (1969) 14: 710–719.

102. Quinn, J. F. Competitive hierarchies in marine benthic communities. *Oecologia* (1982) 54: 129–135.

103. Rigg, G. B., and R. C. Miller. Intertidal plant and animal zonation in the vicinity of Neah Bay, Washington. *Proceedings of the California Academy of Science* (1949) 26: 323–351.

104. Rivest, B. R. Development and the influence of nurse egg allotment on hatching size in *Searlesia dira* (Reeve, 1846) (Prosobranchia: Buccinidae). *Journal of Experimental Marine Biology and Ecology* (1983) 69: 217–241.

105. Roden, G. I. On statistical estimation of monthly extreme sea-surface temperatures along the west coast of the United States. *Journal of Marine Research* (1963) 21(3): 172–190.

106. Russ, G. R. Overgrowth in a marine epifaunal community: Competitive hierarchies and competitive networks. *Oecologia* (1982) 53: 12–19.

107. Scagel, R. F. *An investigation on marine plants near Hardy Bay, B.C.,* 1. Victoria, B.C.: Provincial Department of Fisheries, 1947.

108. Scheltema, R. The dispersal of the larvae of shoal-water benthic invertebrate species over long distances by ocean currents. In D. J. Crisp (Ed.), *European Marine Biology Symposium* (vol. 4). New York: Cambridge University Press, 1971.

109. Sebens, K. P. The allometry of feeding, energetics, and body size in three sea anemone species. *Biological Bulletin* (1981) 161: 152–171.

110. Sebens, K. P. Recruitment and habitat selection in the intertidal sea anemones *Anthopleura elegantissima* (Brandt) and *A. xanthogrammica* (Brandt). *Journal of Experimental Marine Biology and Ecology* (1982) 59: 103–124.

111. Sebens, K. P. The limits to indeterminate growth: An optimal size model applied to passive suspension feeders. *Ecology* (1982) 63(1): 209–222.

112. Sebens, K. P. Population dynamics and habitat suitability of the intertidal sea anemones *Anthopleura elegantissima* and *A. xanthogrammica*. *Ecological Monographs* (1983) 53(4): 405–433.

113. Slocum, C. J. Differential susceptibility to grazers in two phases of an intertidal alga: Advantages of heteromorphic generations. *Journal of Experimental Marine Biology and Ecology* (1980) 46: 99–110.

114. Sousa, W. P. Disturbance in marine intertidal boulder fields: The nonequilibrium maintenance of species diversity. *Ecology* (1979) 60(6): 1225–1239.

115. Spight, T. M. Hatching size and the distribution of nurse eggs among Prosobranch embryos. *Biological Bulletin* (1976) 150: 491–499.

116. Steneck, R. S. A limpet-coralline alga association: Adaptations and defenses between a selective herbivore and its prey. *Ecology* (1982) 63: 502–522.

117. Steneck, R. S. Escalating herbivory and resulting adaptive trends in calcareous algal crusts. *Paleobiology* (1983) 9(1): 44–61.

118. Stevenson, J. C. Recovery potential of oiled marine northern environments. *Journal of the Fisheries Research Board of Canada* (1978) 35(5): 499–796.

119. Strathmann, R. R. The spread of sibling larvae of sedentary marine invertebrates. *American Naturalist* (1974) 108(959): 29–44.

120. Strathmann, R. R., E. S. Branscomb, and K. Vedder. Fatal errors in set as a cost of dispersal and the influence of intertidal flora on set of barnacles. *Oecologia* (1981) 48: 13–18.

121. Suchanek, T. H. The role of disturbance in the evolution of life history strategies in the intertidal mussels *Mytilus edulis* and *Mytilus californianus*. *Oecologia* (1981) 50: 143–152.

122. Taylor, P. R., and M. M. Littler. The roles of compensatory morality, physical disturbance, and substrate retention in the development and organization of a sand-influenced, rocky intertidal community. *Ecology* (1982) 63(1): 135–146.

123. Tegner, M. J., and P. K. Dayton. Sea urchins recruitment patterns and implications of commercial fishing. *Science* (1977) 196: 324–326.

124. Trapp, J. L. Variations in summer diet of glaucus-winged gulls in the Western Aleutian Islands: an ecological interpretation. *Wilson Bulletin* (1979) 91: 412–419.

125. Turner, T. Facilitation as a successional mechanism in a rocky intertidal community. *American Naturalist* (1983) 121: 729–738.

126. Vadas, R. L. Preferential feeding: An optimization strategy in sea urchins. *Ecological Monographs* (1977) 47: 337–371.

127. Vance, R. R. Competition and mechanism of coexistence in three sympatric species of intertidal hermit crabs. *Ecology* (1972) 53: 1062–1074.

128. Vance, R. R. The role of shell adequacy in behavioral interactions involving hermit crabs. *Ecology* (1972) 53: 1075–1083.

129. Vine, P. J. Effects of algal grazing and aggressive behavior of the fishes *Pomacentrus lividus* and *Acanthurus sohal* on coral-reef ecology. *Marine Biology* (1974) 24: 131–136.

130. Wagner, R. H., D. W. Phillips, J. D. Standing, and C. Hand. Commensalism or mutualism: Attraction of a sea star towards its symbiotic polychaete. *Journal of Experimental Marine Biology and Ecology* (1979) 39: 205–210.

131. Whittaker, R. H. *Communities and Ecosystems* (second edition). New York and London: Macmillan, 1975.

132. Woodin, S. A. Refuges, disturbance, and community structure: A marine soft-bottom example. *Ecology* (1978) 59(2): 274–284.

III

Plate Number: Reference Numbers in Lists I & II

1: 14, 64, & 105
2a & 2b: 4 & 12
3: 30, 80, 107, & 131
4: 8, 37, & 69
7: 6, 7, & 12
10: 37, 95, & 103
11: 83, 93, & 95
14: 28, 34, 93, & 114
17: 63, 127, & 128
19a & 19b: 55, 56, & 73
20: 92
21: 28, 29, & 34
22: 61, 67, 93, 98, & 121

23a & 23b: 68, 102, & 106
25: 22, 54, & 91
28: 36 & 96
30: 122
31a & 31b: 34 & 100
32a & 32b: 7, 8, 11, 39, 64, 77, & 103
35: 10, 25, & 32
36: 35, 111, & 112
37: 109
38a: 90
38b & 38c: 76 & 79
39: 4, 50, 72, 83, 94, & 97
40a & 40b: 4 & 34
41: 18, 75, & 117

42a, 42b, & 42c: 21, 40, 44, 48, 49, 76, 101, 126, & 129
43: 46, 66, & 132
44: 81 & 82
45 & 46: 47
47: 91 & 130
48: 21, 24, 76, & 89
48: 57, 62, & 124
49a & 49b: 78, 99, & 113
51: 38 & 125
53: 116 & 117
54a & 54b: 70 & 107
56b: 108 & 119

57a & 57b: 55, 56, & 111
58: 20, 26, 41, 42, 60, 85, & 86
59a & 59b: 104 & 115
60: 36 & 96
63: 33, 65, & 120
65: 44 & 123
67: 51
69: 59
71: 23
77: 27, 45, & 74
78: 51, 72, & 95
80: 52
81: 31
82: 32 & 84
89: 87

Photographic Sites

1: Tatoosh Island, Washington, 6/82; 2a & 2b: Tatoosh Island, Washington, 7/81; 3: Tatoosh Island, Washington, 5/80; 4: Tatoosh Island, Washington, 6/79; 5: Tatoosh Island, Washington, 5/82; 34: Tatoosh Island, Washington, 4/82; 7: Tatoosh Island, Washington, 6/79; 8: Tatoosh Island, Washington, 6/84; 9: Tatoosh Island, Washington, 7/83; 10: Tatoosh Island, Washington, 6/84; 11: Duk Point, Washington, 2/80; 12a: Tatoosh Island, Washington, 4/83; 12b: Tatoosh Island, Washington, 5/83; 12c: Noarlunga, Australia, 4/82; 13: Tatoosh Island, Washington, 4/80; 14: Tatoosh Island, Washington, 7/83; 15: Torch Bay, Alaska, 7/81; 16a: Salt Point, California, 7/76; 16b: Tatoosh Island, Washington, 7/80; 16c: Tatoosh Island, Washington, 6/80; 17: Tatoosh Island, Washington, 5/83; 18: Torch Bay, Alaska, 7/81; 19a: Tatoosh Island, Washington, 5/83; 19b: Pierce Point, California, 5/83; 20: Tatoosh Island, Washington, 9/79; 21: Tatoosh Island, Washington, 9/79; 22: Tatoosh Island, Washington, 8/82; 23a: Torch Bay, Alaska, 7/80; 23b: Torch Bay, Alaska, 8/81; 24: Tatoosh Island, Washington, 6/82; 25: Tatoosh Island, Washington, 6/81; 26: Tatoosh Island, Washington, 6/81; 27: Tatoosh Island, Washington, 4/83; 28: Tatoosh Island, Washington, 6/83; 29: Pierce Point, California, 7/75; 30: Duk Point, Washington, 2/80; 31a: Tatoosh Island, Washington, 2/81; 31b: Tatoosh Island, Washington, 6/83; 32a: Tatoosh Island, Washington, 5/82; 32b: Seal Rock, Washington, 6/81; 33a: Tatoosh

Island, Washington, 6/80; 33b: Tatoosh Island, Washington, 7/81; 61: Tatoosh Island, Washington, 4/83; 35: Tatoosh Island, Washington, 6/80; 36: Tatoosh Island, Washington, 7/81; 37: Seal Rock, Washington, 5/81; 38b: Waadah Island, Washington, 5/80; 38c: Waadah Island, Washington, 5/78; 38a: Point Lobos, California, 11/76; 39: Tatoosh Island, Washington, 6/82; 40a: Torch Bay, Alaska, 6/81; 40b: Torch Bay, Alaska, 6/81; 41: Tatoosh Island, Washington, 8/82; 42c & 42a: Tatoosh Island, Washington, 6/81; 42b: Tatoosh Island, Washington, 6/81; 48: Salt Point, California 5/75; 43: Point Lobos, California, 11/76; 44: Tatoosh Island, Washington, 6/82; 45 & 46: Tatoosh Island, Washington, 6/82; 47: Tatoosh Island, Washington, 3/80; 48: Tatoosh Island, Washington, 7/83; 49a: Portage Head, Washington, 6/81; 49b: Portage Head, Washington, 6/81; 50: Tatoosh Island, Washington, 8/80; 51: Tatoosh Island, Washington, 8/82; 52: Tatoosh Island, Washington, 5/82; 53: Tatoosh Island, Washington, 7/80; 54a: Tatoosh Island, Washington, 8/84; 54b: Tatoosh Island, Washington, 2/84; 55a: Tatoosh Island, Washington, 6/81; 55b: Torch Bay, Alaska, 7/80; 55c: Tatoosh Island, Washington, 7/81; 56: Pile Point, San Juan Island, Washington, 4/79; 57a: Tatoosh Island, Washington, 8/82; 57b: Tatoosh Island, Washington, 8/79; 58: Tatoosh Island, Washington, 4/84; 59a: Botanical Beach, Vancouver Island, British Columbia, 7/79; 60: Tatoosh Island, Washington, 6/82; 61: Tatoosh Island, Washington, 7/83; 62: Tatoosh Island, Washington, 7/82; 73: Tatoosh Island, Washington, 7/84; 63: Torch Bay, Alaska, 8/83; 64: Tatoosh Island, Washington, 7/83; 65: Tatoosh Island, Washington, 5/81; 66: Tatoosh Island, Washington, 7/83; 56a: Tatoosh Island, Washington, 7/83; 68: Tatoosh Island, Washington, 8/84; 69: Pierce Point, California, 5/75; 70: Torch Bay, Alaska, 8/81; 71: Botanical Beach, Vancouver Island, British Columbia, 7/79; 72: Pierce Point, California, 7/75; 22a: Tatoosh Island, Washington, 8/84; 74: Tatoosh Island, Washington, 5/84; 75: Pierce Point, California, 6/75; 67: Tatoosh Island, Washington, 7/81; 77: Tatoosh Island, Washington, 5/83; 78: Tatoosh Island, Washington, 6/83; 79: James Fitzgerald Marine Reserve, California, 6/76; 80: Tatoosh Island, Washington, 6/79; 81: Tatoosh Island, Washington, 7/83; 82: Pierce Point, California, 5/75; 83: Torch Bay, Alaska, 7/81; 84: Tatoosh Island, Washington, 5/84; 85a: Tatoosh Island, Washington, 7/79; 85b: Pierce Point, California, 8/76; 86: Tatoosh Island, Washington, 7/80; 87: Tatoosh Island, Washington, 6/82; 88: Tatoosh Island, Washington, 6/80; 89: Tatoosh Island, Washington, 6/80; 90: Tatoosh Island, Washington, 5/80; 76: Tatoosh Island, Washington, 8/79; 92: Tatoosh Island, Washington, 5/82.

Index

155